THE NATURE OF SCIENCE

THE
NATURE
OF
SCIENCE

AND OTHER ESSAYS

by

DAVID GREENWOOD

FOREWORD by ROSGYLL AYRES

KENNIKAT PRESS
Port Washington, N. Y./London

B
840
.G68
1971

THE NATURE OF SCIENCE

Copyright, 1959, by Philosophical Library, Inc.
Reissued in 1971 by Kennikat Press by arrangement
Library of Congress Catalog Card No: 79-122863
ISBN 0-8046-1408-3

Manufactured by Taylor Publishing Company   Dallas, Texas

ESSAY AND GENERAL LITERATURE INDEX REPRINT SERIES

To the Members
of the
Los Angeles Centre
of the
Royal Institute of Philosophy

λαμπάδια ἔχοντες διαδώσουσιν ἀλλήλοις.
—PLATO, *Republic.*

FOREWORD
by
ROSGYLL AYRES
Formerly Professor of Physics,
Cairo University

This book is an attempt to tackle a few of the most pressing problems in the foundations of science. The emphasis throughout is on the *linguistic* aspects of science and mathematics, and should be of particular interest to those who, though not scientists themselves, are concerned with the application of the most recent theories of syntax and semantics to the language of modern science.

Throughout his discussions, the author reinforces his earlier published views on the *formalization* of science. This method of approach has caused much discussion in the past, particularly as opposed to "intuitive" methods. When abstract, nonintuitive formulas, such as Maxwell's equations of electromagnetism, were first proposed as new axioms, some physicists endeavored to make them "intuitive" by constructing a "model," i.e., a way of representing electromagnetic microprocesses by an analogy to known macroprocesses, such as the movements of visible things. But it is important to bear in mind that the discovery of a model has only an aesthetic or heuristic value, and is not essential for the successful application of a scientific theory. As the special character of scientific theories tends to be given them more and more by mathematics, it may be assumed that the tendency towards formalization will increase. In this way we may arrive eventually at a unity of science embracing all known mathematical laws.

Sometimes the author indicates his standpoint independently of the conflicting positions which he is discussing, and sometimes he adopts the opinion of one of the disputants. Inevitably not everybody will agree with him entirely, but few can fail to be stimulated. Both philosophers and scientists can derive benefit from these essays, even though quantum theory has upset the foundations of science and there is no general agreement on the style of the new foundations. David Greenwood has illumined some of the most controversial areas of the philosophy of science, and has thereby performed a service which should prove valuable and constructive.

TABLE OF CONTENTS

PREFACE

This book is intended as a collection of five essays in the general area of logic and mathematics as applied to science, composed, at various times, during the course of the past decade. The development of the methods and results of natural science is possibly the most significant intellectual contribution of modern western civilization to the galaxy of man's supreme achievements. I use the term "natural science" in its widest sense, including all theoretical knowledge which cannot by definition be included under the category of the divine sciences, and which comprehends knowledge both discovered by the application of special scientific procedures and based on common sense in everyday life. In the same way the expression "language of science" is meant here to refer to the language which contains all statements, i.e., theoretical sentences, in contradistinction to emotional expressions, commands, etc., used for scientific purposes in everyday life. What is usually called science I take to be a more systematic continuation of those activities which we carry out in everyday life in order to learn more about the world around us.

As in my earlier book *Truth and Meaning*, I have not distinguished between any special logic of the empirical sciences and logic in general, since I doubt if any such differentiation really exists. I have taken logic as the name of the discipline which analyzes the meaning of the concepts common to all the sciences, and establishes the general laws governing the concepts. But I do recognize two chief parts of the analysis of linguistic expressions in science. Scientific investigation may be restricted to the forms of the linguistic expressions involved and their relation to objects outside of language. An investigation of this type comes within the field of logical syntax, is restricted to formal analysis and abstracts from designation. In the second case, an investigation may not be restricted to formal analysis, but may take designation into consideration. An investigation of this type comes within the field of semantics, and includes the semantical analysis of the designation of expressions. It will be obvious that this second part of scientific analysis is considerably broader than the first. A further distinction should be made between formal science and empirical science. Formal science consists of analytic statements established by logic and mathematics; empirical science consists of synthetic statements established in the different fields of factual knowledge.

Although in actual scientific practice the processes of framing a theoretical substructure and of providing it with an interpretation are not always sharply separated, since the intended interpretation usually guides the construction of the theorist, I accept it as possible, for the purposes of logical clarification, to separate the two steps conceptually. A theoretical system in physics may be conceived as an uninterpreted theory in axiomatic form. This is characterized by a specified set of primitive terms and postulates. The primitive terms are not defined within the theory, and all other extra-logical terms of the theory are obtained from them by nominal definition. The postulates are primitive hypotheses and other sentences of the theory are obtained from them by logical deduction. It should be noted that the conception of physical theories as presented in axiomatized form is an idealization made for purposes of logical clarification and rational construction. Actual attempts to axiomatize theories of empirical science have so far been rare (one immediately remembers the work of Reichenbach, Walker, Woodger, Hull and a few others) but the general principles of axiomatization are accepted by large numbers of philosophers and scientists.

My gratitude is due to many persons. Professor Rudolf Carnap and Bertrand Russell, two of my former teachers, have taken a generous interest in the progress of these essays. The helpful advice of many distinguished members of the Rand Corporation at Santa Monica, California, and of North American Aviation, Inc. was always available to me. Dr. Peter Hodgson of the Department of Physics, University College, London, read and discussed an early draft of the manuscript, and Professor Carl Spurney of Marymount College, Los Angeles, provided great assistance with the preparation of the text for publication.

This brief work was concluded in my capacity of Senior Research Analyst in the California Institute of Technology. I am especially grateful to many colleagues in the Institute who provided opinions and suggestions, and especially to the President, Dr. Lee DuBridge, who was always hard pressed by problems of more than theoretical importance. Dr. Michael Wermel was particularly gracious in providing specialized help during the final stages of editing, and the staff of the Institute Library worked their customary quiet wonders.

David Greenwood

California Institute of Technology,
Pasadena

I

THE NATURE OF SCIENCE

Any present-day philosophical outlook on life is, broadly speaking, a product of two streams of development—one, inherited religious and theological conceptions; the other, the sort of investigation which may be entitled "scientific" in the broadest sense of that much-abused word. Philosophy, as I understand the title, is intermediate between theology and science. Scientific knowledge is by definition restricted to what is empirical and testable; theological knowledge, though based on a rational foundation, has developed vast superstructures which are finally provable only with recourse to divine revelation or ecclesiastical traditions, neither of which forms a part of normal scientific procedure. Between the scientist and the theologian there is a No Man's Land occupied by the philosopher. Though he is open to attack from both of his vigorous neighbors, he is in the best position to appreciate the theoretical substructures underlying the imposing syntheses which have been erected on each side of him.

The Greek thinkers never explicitly distinguished between the natural sciences and the philosophy of nature. Indeed, the word *science* in its more ancient and comprehensive sense includes both philosophy and what is today called science. In this older and broader sense, science means knowledge that is certain because the reasons of its truth are known. The reasons with which the knowledge is concerned may be primary or secondary causes, real causes of the order of substantial being or regular antecedents of the phenomenal order. Where the causes are primary, real, and of the order of substances, the certain knowledge of them is philosophy. Where the causes are secondary, simply logical and of the order of phenomena, the certain knowledge of them is science, in the modern, narrower sense of the term.

The dividing line between science and philosophy is difficult to

1

draw exactly. Both begin with phenomena which are sensibly observable, since all knowledge has its origin in sense perception. But the method of philosophy is to proceed from the observable phenomena to the real causes which underlie the phenomena, while the method of science is to proceed from the observable phenomena to a formula expressing a regular order in the occurrences of the phenomena, and eventually, through the application of this formula, to the prediction of future phenomena. An example will clarify this distinction. Both philosopher and scientist observe that elementary substances in nature unite to form compound substances. From this fact the philosopher reasons to the conclusion that corporeal substances are essentially constituted by a determinable, potential principle which is the same in all of them, and a determining actual principle which is specifically different in all of them. The scientist, on the other hand, after examining a great number of such combinations, and applying exact measurements to the substances involved in them, formulates laws of chemical affinity and of the combined weights of elements, and makes probable predictions for the future. Both the philosopher and the scientist study being which is sensible and motile. The philosopher gives stress to *being*, and studies corporeal substance under the aspect of its real or ontological essence and causes. The sensible qualities of the object are the data for the mind's activity, and not its goals. The scientist gives stress to *sensible and motile*, subordinating being to sensible quality, identifying substances with their observable properties, and not primarily concerning himself with the non-observable, non-physical aspects of material phenomena.

I assume as axiomatic that every scientific theory is a system of sentences which are accepted as true and which may be categorized under the title of laws or statements. I further assume that science as a whole may be divided into two sub-disciplines: the factual sciences, embracing the totality of all purely empirical disciplines, and the formal sciences, embracing all non-empirical disciplines, of which logic is the corner stone. This difference is based on my belief in the syntactical and semantical dichotomy between analytic and synthetic statements. A statement is analytic if it is unconditionally valid according to the transformation rules which determine under what conditions a statement is a consequence of other statements.

Its validity should be independent of the truth or falsity of other statements, and it should be a consequence of the null class of statements. A statement is inconsistent if it is unconditionally invalid, that is, if every statement of the language is a consequence of it. A statement is determinate if it is either analytic or inconsistent, and synthetic if it is neither analytic nor inconsistent. A statement is logical if it contains only logical signs, and descriptive if it contains at least one descriptive sign. While all synthetic statements are descriptive, the converse does not hold good. The range of descriptive sentences is always wider than that of synthetic statements.

It is now possible to draw a clear distinction between formal and factual sciences. Formal sciences contain only analytic statements while factual sciences contain only synthetic statements. Analytic statements are of three kinds. Descriptive analytic statements are in close relationship to the factual sciences since they contain descriptive signs, but in a form that permits the question as to whether such statements are true or false to be answered independently of the nature of these entities on the basis of the transformation rules of language. Analytical logical statements and analytical mathematical statements have virtually no difference between them save that the latter contain numerals or predicates relating to numerals.

There is no reason, *prima facie*, why the language of science need contain analytic statements to be sufficient. Synthetic statements should suffice for the formulation of any particular assertion and of general laws, without diminishing the content of science. But while the utilization of only synthetic statements is possible for the construction of the language of science, it is inexpedient and savors of artificiality. I therefore prefer to add to the use of synthetic statements the analytic and inconsistent categories. These latter two groups of statements have no factual content, nor do they express any matters of fact, actual or non-actual, but they serve rather as calculational devices.

In practice, of course, both synthetic and analytic statements are used in the language of science. The factual sciences utilize synthetic statements for the description of any observable facts or general statements which are introduced as hypotheses and used in a tentative manner. Having once established such statements, scientists proceed to the derivation of other synthetic statements, frequently with a view to making predictions about future events. Analytic statements serve in an auxiliary capacity for these inferential functions. Formal science, considered from the viewpoint of the total language, is virtually an auxiliary calculus for dealing with synthetic statements and has no independent significance whatsoever. Its principal importance lies in its ability to perform as an auxiliary component to facilitate linguistic transformations in the factual sciences.

My position is not in the least intended to belittle the importance of formal science. Indeed, by delineating its capacity, I have indirectly emphasized that the logical function of the formal sciences as an auxiliary calculus is compatible with the psychological fact that it is only on occasions that research in any branch of the formal sciences has a possible application in the factual sciences. In adjoining formal and factual sciences, no new area of subject matter is constituted, since the formal sciences do not have any objects at all, being systems of auxiliary statements without either objects or content. This dichotomy between the two types of sciences has therefore no effect on the fundamental unity of science.

The meaning of a statement consists in its expressing a thinkable, though not necessarily an actual, state of affairs. If an alleged statement expresses no thinkable state of affairs, it is meaningless, even though it may yield a meaning in terms of grammatical structure. If a statement expresses a state of affairs, it is meaningful. It is true if this state of affairs exists and false if it does not. It is perfectly possible to know whether a statement is meaningful before knowing whether it is true or false. If a statement contains only concepts which are already known or recognized, it derives its meaning from these. On the other hand, if a statement contains a new concept or one whose scientific applicability is in question, its meaning should be specified. To do this, it is sufficient to state the thinkable experiential situations in which it would be called true, and those in which it would be called false.

Statements in factual sciences must be founded on experience, otherwise they are meaningless. This means that the objects of these sciences must be constituted in such a way that every statement can be translated into a founded statement that has the same truth-value as the original one. To constitute an object implies the formulation of a general rule indicating the way in which a statement containing the name of the first object may be replaced by an equivalent statement not containing it. This general rule finds its most perfect expression in a constitutional definition, of which there are two types, explicit and contextual. An explicit definition is most applicable to simple cases and consists of a rule maintaining that whenever the name of the first object appears, a certain expression containing the names of other objects, but not that of the first object, be substituted for it. A contextual definition consists of a rule of transformation stating generally how statements in which the expression which is not explicitly definable occurs may be replaced by other statements where it does not occur. Constitutional definitions concern only extensions, so that in every statement about a propositional function, the propositional function should be replaced by its sign of extension.

Since neither the formal nor the factual sciences consistently use the logistic language in which constitutional definitions have, of necessity, to be formulated, I propose the use of Carnap's criterion of reducibility in realistic formulation:

"We call an object a 'reducible to objects b, c . . .' if for the existence of every state of affairs with regard to a, b, c . . . a *necessary and sufficient condition* may be given which depends only on objects b, c . . ." (1)

By means of this criterion it is possible to discover whether a given object is capable of being reduced to another object or not. One can thus ascertain the order in which the objects must be constituted to form a connected and comprehensive system of constitution. Since this criterion of reducibility does not uniquely determine the order on every point, I also propose the use of Carnap's principle of epistemological priority, which is defined thus:

"One object (or type of object) is called epistemologically prior with respect to another if the second is known by means of the first and, therefore, knowing the first object is a precondition to the knowledge of the second object." (2)

There would seem to be four main kinds of objects: cultural objects, other minds, physical objects and the data of our own minds. Reducibility is possible in this order, so that cultural objects may be reduced to other minds, these to physical objects, and these again to the data of our own minds. Of course, this order of arrangement is not the only possible one. If, for some good reason, it is found expedient, one may well use physical objects as the basic element, since the objects of our mind may be constituted from the brain processes by means of the psychophysical relation. Physical objects are the material objects of everyday life, which are characterized by filling a certain part of space between two fixed points in time, and possessing at least one sense quality, e.g., color, weight, temperature, etc. There is one fundamental difference between the physical world and the world of perception: while the former is constituted by the attribution of numbers, the physical qualities, the latter is constituted by the attribution of sense-qualities to the world-points. This makes it possible to formulate laws mathematically and to achieve and maintain a unique noncontradictory intersubjectivation.

There appears no valid reason why the totality of statements about objects forming the subject matter of the various sciences should not be capable of being transformed into statements about immediate experiences having the same truth-values as the original statements. All scientific statements are capable of being confirmed or disconfirmed by means of immediate experiences. Only statements consisting solely of logical constants and terms capable of being constituted on the basis of experience are meaningful in the strict sense of the language of science.

A theoretical system which has no factual interpretation and is incapable of test cannot possibly constitute a theory of empirical phenomena, since both its terms and its concepts lack empirical import. Neovitalism, for example, is incapable of an interpretation of its principal term "entelechy," and of terms definable by means of it. Furthermore, it offers no indirect interpretation by formulating a system of general laws and definitions which would connect the term "entelechy" with other, interpreted terms of the theory. A concept can have explanatory power only in the context of an interpreted theory. For example, to maintain that the regularities of planetary motion can be explained by means of the concept of universal gravitation is saying, elliptically, that those regularities are explicable by means of the formal theory of gravitation, together with the usual interpretation of its terms. No term of factual science can be significant unless it possesses an empirical interpretation.

6

I am indebted to the work of the physicist P. W. Bridgman for a further basic concept in scientific thinking, that there must exist, for the terms of factual science, criteria of application couched in terms of observational or experimental procedure. Bridgman asks that "the demand that the concepts or terms used in the description of experience be framed in terms of operations which can be unequivocally performed."(3) This idea, however, should not be confined to merely quantitive terms. The operational criteria of application for the word 'fever,' for example, might be formulated in terms of the various symptoms of fever. These would include not only symptoms known by direct observation of the patient, but also the results of bacteriological tests calling for the use of microscopes and the application of various types of staining techniques.

Factual science as a whole may be divided into two sub-categories, physics and biology, each of these terms interpreted in its broadest sense. The distinction between these two has to be based on the distinction between organisms and nonorganisms in nature. Biology is the study of organisms and physics is the study of nonorganisms. Physics includes chemistry, astronomy, geography, etc., and the sublanguage of the language of science which contains all and only physical terms may be called physical language. Such of these statements which are formulated in the physical language and have a universal appeal are called physical laws. These physical laws are needed for the explanation of processes in inorganic nature, but they also apply to processes in organisms. For this reason biology presupposes physics but not *vice versa*.

The old distinction between physical and bodily processes had its origin in metaphysical mind-body dualism, but the distinction is still a perfectly valid differentiation of the two main branches of biology, even for those who do not admit metaphysical dualism. In the category of bodily processes one may include biology proper, botany, zoology, genetics and animal evolution. The terms which are used in this category, in addition to logical and physical terms, may simply be called biological terms, but the biological language must contain the physical language as a sublanguage. Biological statements and biological laws are formulated in a way analogous to the formulation of physical statements and laws. The second field includes psychology, sociology, etc., but is more vaguely delineated. It is easy to see that every term in the so-called social sciences is reducible to terms of the other fields. The result of any investigation of a group of men of women can be described in terms of their members, their relations to one another or their environment. The human family may be considered as an organism in biology, and indeed is frequently treated in this light by contemporary methodologists, sociologists and sociometrists.

It will be seen, then, that though science has no unity of laws, it does have unity of language, i.e., a common reduction basis for the terms of all branches of science. This basis consists of a very narrow and homogeneous class of terms of the physical thing-language. For many decisions, both in business and social life, predictions must be made on a combined knowledge of the general laws belonging to different branches of science. If the terms of different branches had no logical connection between them, such as is supplied by the homogeneous reduction basis, it would not be possible to connect statements and laws of different fields in such a way as to be able to derive predictions from them. I take it that the unity of the language of science is the basis for practical application of theoretical knowledge.

It does not seem necessary that philosophical postulates should exist for the purposes of initial discussion. Any proposed scientific assertion concerning the order and structure of the universe, no matter how fundamental its role or comprehensive its scope, must be regarded as tentative. Any assertion regarding nature, if it is to be scientifically meaningful, must in principle be testable and consequently confirmable or disconfirmable.

It is requisite that unconfirmable presuppositions should be allowed for the very confirmation of any scientific law. This requirement, which is sometimes referred to as the Presupposition Theory of Induction, is entitled to more general recognition than it has so far received. Burks(4) has been its principal protagonist most recently, but though I admire his work, I cannot feel otherwise than that it is only a beginning. He admits that the problem is insoluble in its traditional frame of reference since Hume, because it involves a *petitio principii.* If we attempt to transform induction into deduction, necessarily we require premises whose validity is inductive, and if we try to prove the probable success of inductive inference

8

on the basis of its prior success, we assume the very principle which we are supposed to be proving. Burks' standpoint is that the presuppositions of induction result in the choice of a definition of a concept of degree of confirmation which bestows certainty upon its own presuppositions once it is adopted, and a probability of zero to any alternative presupposition.

The first thought that occurs to mind in considering Burks' analysis is that since he is unable to decide with certainty which presuppositional analysis actually applies to this universe, what is the point of any scientist's attempting to make the same decision? An answer, by way of using a different approach, has been propounded independently by Carnap and Reichenbach. The normal method of induction is part of Carnap's definition of a logical concept of probability. Carnap's degree of confirmation, like Keynes' concept of probability, is relational in that it determines the degree to which some specific piece of given evidence supports an inductive conclusion. Reichenbach proposes a concept of *weight* for singular predictive inferences as well as for the probability of hypotheses. These two theories of probability, though they differ considerably, are related by the fact that the supporting evidence in Carnap's conception consists in observed frequency ratios, while Reichenbach's concept of weight is defined similarly in terms of the relative frequency of a certain type of event in a properly chosen reference class. According to Carnap there is a continuum of inductive rules, in which Reichenbach's conception has its place, all of which have this feature in common that, if the world has any degree of order at all, predictions made according to any one of the inductive rules will ultimately converge with the others. Furthermore, these rules can be shown deductively to be the only type of predictions that utilize evidence methodically and are capable of anticipating the order of natural phenomena.

While recognizing the value of Burks' work, I suggest the following tentative riders to his conclusions:

(1) The procedure of normal induction is the only methodological procedure of which we can prove deductively that it can disclose the uniformities in our world.

(2) Through the manifestations of the principle of induction, we

9

observe that our world contains a great deal of nonuniformity and a small amount of uniformity, e.g. causal and statistical orders. This assumption, which is inductively established, could serve as an initial postulate, but is not metaphysical in the sense of being *a priori*.

(3) Inductive methods such as R. A. Fisher's method of maximum likelihood, Carnap's definition of degree of confirmation c^* and Reichenbach's rule of induction provide virtually equivalent results in the long run. Perhaps they are variations of the same fundamental principle. This principle may be stated thus: If we want a method of generalization or of individual predictive inference that makes use of evidence and yields unique results, the normal methods are always preferable to the perverse varieties. These latter are either insensitive to the testimony of accumulating evidence or they lack the uniqueness that typifies the methods of simplest generalization or of maximum likelihood.

(4) When deciding the most adequate value for the limiting frequency of statistical phenomena (e.g. radioactive disintegration, Mendelian inheritance, etc.), there are two procedures from which to choose. The first is straight-line generalization of the statistical ratios obtaining for specifiable aspects under operationally identifiable conditions; the second, the construction of a theory containing assumptions regarding statistical distributions, in such a way that the observed data will have a maximum likelihood in the light of the assumed theoretical model.

As a result of the abandonment of the former scientific dogma of determinism, the problem of probability has come to have the same place of importance formerly occupied by determinism. Kneale(5) has gone as far as to indicate that the principal business of the philosopher is to clarify the meaning of probability statements made by plain men, and to some extent the same remark could be made of the scientist. I have discussed the question of probability statements in *Truth and Meaning*, and so with my earlier conclusions in mind I will attempt to relate probability statements with the process of inductive decisions normally practised (willingly or not) by scientists.

When tracing the steps in any argument from observation to induction, it is first of all requisite to guarantee that the observations are in harmony with our existing knowledge. In any experiment or observational inquiry, it is in principle possible to say whether the results are in agreement or in more or less strong disagreement with existing knowledge. If a mistake occurs, it may be explained on one of three grounds:

(1) A mistake has been made in carrying out the experiment or recording the observations.
(2) The existing knowledge is wrong and needs to be modified.
(3) A mistake has occurred in deductive reasoning.

If no noticeable disagreement exists between what is observed and existing knowledge, we are in a position to consider the hypotheses possible in the light of the observations, with due regard to prior confidence derived from analogy and previous experience that the truth lies in some range between a willingness-to-consider and a strong expectation close to "knowledge." If several hypotheses are considered, all of them will have a separate prior confidence. Confidences are vague in relative magnitude, but if the inductive reasoning connected with them were formalised, there would not be any obvious inadequacy in postulating a numerical distribution of prior confidence as an additive set function whose value for the whole field of hypothesis is unity. We should also pay heed, when occasion arises, to the risk of wasting time or money in cases where a hypothesis is accepted as true and turns out eventually to be untrue. Risks are also vague in magnitude, but a complete numerical risk-function could almost certainly be formulated in a formal theory.(6)

Kneale has suggested that the practice of induction consists of following the principle usually referred to by statisticians as the method of maximum likelihood. This particular principle is, however, not always applicable. Not all induction problems can be framed as problems of estimation. For example, in the case of testing the adequacy of fit of a specified theoretical probability model, the

11

relevant statistical tool is a test of significance, and not an estimate. Furthermore, there is always an assumption in supposing that a constant being estimated really is a constant. In speaking of P (a, b), the frequency-probability that an a thing is a b thing, we assume that b-ness is distributed over a-ness in such a way that it is adequately described by a fixed probability law. But not all random phenomena can be described in terms of fixed probabilities, variation in biology being particularly irregular. Furthermore, a single estimate of the constant, such as is given by the maximum likelihood or any other method of point-estimation, is not likely to be adequate even if we are satisfied that a simple probability model is suitable for describing the observations, and we propose to estimate an unknown constant in the model. We must know how accurate the estimate is likely to be. There are several ways of assessing the accuracy of the estimate, e.g.:

(1) Estimating the error variance between an estimate of the unknown constant in which we are interested and an estimate of the accuracy of this first estimate,
(2) Using an interval estimate instead of a point estimate, and working with a pair of values known as "confidence limits," close together and such that we may place a known high degree of confidence in the assertion that the unknown constant lies between them.

At least one of these methods should be applicable in most cases.

It cannot be too strongly emphasized that the most which the philosopher or scientist can derive from such procedures as I have indicated is a greater or lesser degree of probability. There is no possibility of infallible prediction on purely empirical premises. Indeed, I propose to advance this argument one stage further, and manifest that no scientific proof of the existence of unexperienced objects is possible. Obviously any supposed reasoning could not be inductive. Induction is generalisation from observed facts, but there is no single proven case of an unexperienced existence having been observed on which could be based the generalization that entities continue to exist when no one is experiencing them. In like manner, there is not a single known instance of the existence of an unex-

perienced entity which could provide the slightest reason for supposing that the paper on which I am writing existed in the past or
will exist in the future when nobody experiences it.

The required inference must be of a formal, deductive nature,
since inductive reasoning is not applicable here. If I wish to show
that a deductive inference can be drawn from the existence of this
paper now, as I experience it, to its existence when nobody experiences it, this means that to assert together the two propositions:

(1) that it exists now, and
(2) that it does not exist when nobody experiences it,

is an internally inconsistent proposition. In fact, there is absolutely
no inconsistency between these propositions. There is nothing internally inconsistent in the view that nothing whatever exists, or has
existed, or will exist, except my own personal sense-data. The possibility that nobody has ever held this view does not make it inconsistent. Therefore, no deductive inference whatsoever can prove the
existence of an unexperienced entity. It is therefore not possible to
prove the existence of such an entity by either inductive or deductive
procedures.

While we *believe* that things exist when we do not observe them,
there is no scientific proof for their existence during their unobserved periods. And just as we cannot infer from anything which
we experience the existence of unexperienced things, so we cannot
prove the operation of unexperienced processes and laws, e.g. causation. If I go out of the house, leave a fire burning and return later,
there is no evidence to show that the fire went on burning during
my absence. Any supposed inference will be based on the belief
that the law of causation operates continuously through time, whether
observed or unobserved, and this was the very thing that had to be
proved. Any argument attempting to prove the maintenance of burning during my absence will necessarily involve a *petitio principii.*

In concluding these comments on the nature of science, it is hardly
necessary to elaborate on the fact that the special character of
scientific deductions tends more and more to be given them by
mathematics. The consequences of this development are important
for philosophy. Mathematics deals with logical constructs—*entia
rationis* instead of with real being. Therefore, the more a physical

13

science submits itself to mathematics, the more it introduces *entia rationis* into its structure. These rational entities enter into the sciences in the core of their deductive function, since it is by the mathematical formulation of its observations and measurements that a science is able to form mathematically expressed hypotheses, and it is through its hypotheses that a natural science is able to make predictions. The phenomena which the natural sciences study and the order that they discover among these phenomena have real causes, namely the essences which are manifested through the phenomena. The mathematical formulae and laws of the natural sciences do not express these essences, but they derive their validity from them. This view of the function of theories and laws in the natural sciences saves modern physics from the charge that it is not directly concerned with the real world at all. If theories, laws and formulae are taken to function for simple entities and accepted as substitutes for real essences, it is not necessary to conclude that the science embodying them is cut off from the physical world. The law or formula expresses a regular relation between phenomena, and the essence for which the formula is substituted is the cause of this regular relation. However little real connection the formula has with the essence itself, it still expresses a real fact when it expresses the relationship between the phenomena. The *entia rationis* of the natural sciences have a real foundation in the physical order. The mathematical formulae of science are logical beings but the phenomena are real beings. Without this foundation in reality, no sciencific prediction of events in the real order would be of any value.

II

CONCEPT FORMATION AND OPERATIONAL DEFINITION

Among the kinds of concept which are at present in use among scientists, there are three of special significance. These are generally termed classificatory, comparative and quantitative, and they will all be discussed separately.

Classificatory concepts were more frequently used in the days of prescientific thinking, though they still remain useful for the formulation of observational results. Their purpose is to classify things or cases into two or any other small plurality of mutually exclusive kinds. Two examples may be useful in illustrating this type of concept. A metalurgist may divide metals into gold, silver, iron, copper, etc., until he has a complete list of all known classifications of the class of metals. Similarly a biologist may divide animals and plants into classes, orders, families, genera and species. In these cases, the classificatory concepts are properties. Again, I may make a statement such as:

"The person x is acquainted with the field of science y."

In this instance the classificatory concepts are relations, a relation being regarded as a property of ordered pairs.

Generally, a classification of the objects in a given domain D is realized by laying down a set of at least two criteria such that every element of D satisfies exactly one of these criteria. Each criterion determines a particular class, viz. the class of all objects in D which satisfy the criterion. If each object in D satisfies exactly one of the criteria, then the necessary requirements of exclusiveness and exhaustiveness are satisfied, for the classes thus determined are mutually exclusive and jointly exhaustive of D.

Of particular significance for empirical science is the case where at least one of the conditions of exclusiveness and exhaustiveness is satisfied not only as a logical consequence of the determining criteria

15

but as a matter of empirical fact. This instance manifests an empirical law and hence confers a measure of systematic import on the classificatory concepts involved. For example, crystals may be classified on the basis of developments in crystallography, or the animal kingdom may be divided into the classifications of its various species. These divisions are obviously not logically exhaustive, but to the extent that they are factually so, they do have some systematic import in virtue of laws maintaining that every object in the domain under consideration satisfies one of the determining criteria.

Occasionally in the writings of philosophers, one meets a distinction between natural and artificial classifications. The taxonomic division of the animal kingdom into orders, families, genera and species by reference to phylogenetic criteria is said to constitute a natural classification, whereas its division into weight classes would be considered artificial. The difficulty with this type of division is that it is too obscure to be of much use. I have grave doubts as to what extent anyone is justified in speaking of the essential characteristics of an individual thing. The usual interpretation of 'essential characteristic' as a characteristic without which a thing would not be what it is would seem to qualify every characteristic of everything as essential. The concept then becomes almost valueless. Furthermore, if a natural classification is interpreted as one whose defining characteristics have a high systematic import, the distinction between natural and artificial merely becomes one of degree. In any case the extent to which a proposed classification is natural has to be ascertained by empirical investigation. This may well prove that a classification is natural in zoology and artificial in social science and presumably some classifications would be ambiguous in any context. In short, I see little value in the distinction between natural and artificial classifications.

Comparative concepts, occasionally referred to as topological or order concepts, serve for the formulation of the result of a comparison in the form of a statement without using numerical values. A comparative concept is invariably a relation. If the classificatory sub-concept is a property (e.g., strong), the comparative concept is a dyadic relation (e.g., stronger). If the classificatory sub-concept is itself a dyadic relation (e.g., the relation of x being acquainted with the field y), the comparative concept normally has four arguments (e.g., the relation of x being better acquainted with y than v with w). The tetradic relation may perfectly well be regarded as a dyadic relation between two pairs (e.g., the relation of being acquainted holds good for the pair x, y to a higher degree than in the case of the pair v, w). There are circumstances in scientific procedures when the triadic relation is preferable to the tetradic relation. For example, it is possible to state the comparison between Mr. Smith's knowledge of engineering with Mr. Brown's knowledge of physics in two triadic relations expressed by the following phrases: 'Mr. Smith is better acquainted with the field of engineering than with that of physics' or 'Mr. Smith is better acquainted with the field of engineering than Mr. Brown is.' Each of these relations involves something different. The first requires that we should be able to compare the degree of Mr. Smith's knowledge of engineering with his knowledge of physics. The second involves the comparison of Mr. Smith's knowledge of engineering with that of Mr. Brown. Each of these relations will be suitable for different sets of circumstances. But in these cases the comparative concept, regarded as a dyadic relation, has the relational properties of being irreflexive, transitive and asymmetric.

There is yet another type of comparative concept, regarded as a dyadic relation, which is reflexive and transitive but neither symmetric nor asymmetric. With respect to the classificatory sub-concept this further type of comparative concept means 'more or equal' (e.g., the relation of x being at least as strong as y), or 'less or equal' (e.g., the relation of x being at most as strong as y). A comparative relation is sometimes of such a kind that, for any x and y it holds good either between x and y or between y and x, or both, and in this case the relation orders its members in a kind of linear order. If the condition is not fulfilled, there remain incomparable cases.

Some further examples will help in clarifying the comparative concept. If a scientist should wish to establish a concept of mass for the class C_1 of medium-sized bodies, he must specify criteria which determine for any two objects in C_1 whether they have the same mass, or which has the smaller one. Similarly, a comparative concept of strength for the class C_2 of aerodynamic apparati is determined by criteria which specify, for any two elements of C_2, whether they are of equal strength, or which of them is less strong.

17

The elements of the given domain may then be arranged in serial order. If an object has smaller mass or strength than another, it precedes it; if it has the same mass or strength, it coincides with the other.

At this stage the scientist must arrive at some decisions as to how to introduce a comparative concept in regard to some specific application. From the conclusions reached so far in this discussion, it is clear that a comparative concept with the domain of application D may be introduced by specifying criteria of coincidence and precedence for the elements of D in regard to the characteristic to be represented by the concept. The relations C of coincidence and P of precedence must be chosen with a view to arranging the elements of D in a quasi-serial order. Any two elements of D must be comparable with regard to the attribute under consideration, i.e., they must either possess it to the same extent or one must possess it to a lesser extent than the other.(1)

Of the three types of concept under discussion, the quantitative is the most powerful, enabling us to give a more precise description of concrete situations and to formulate more comprehensive general laws. There has been some discussion in the past as to whether the quantitative concept ever occurs in the language of scientists, but I presume its theoretical existence. By way of illustration, I take those concepts which have led to the quantitative concept of speed in mechanics. The state of the motion of bodies with respect to speed can be described in the simplest and most elementary way with the help of classificatory concepts like Quick, Slow and Intermediate stages. Presumably, if what the philologists generally agree upon is correct, there was a stage in the development of language when only the classificatory terms were available. Later, the language became more refined with the introduction of a comparative term like 'quicker' and finally the corresponding quantitative concept of speed was introduced into the language structure. The concept speed may be regarded as an explicatum for the comparative concept quicker, and is defined with reference to a speedometer or some similar measuring instrument.

These three types of concepts may usefully be compared. In contrast to the "either . . . or" character of classificatory concepts, comparative and quantitative procedures allow for a "more or less" type

18

of gradual transition from cases where the characteristic they represent is virtually absent to others where it is well pronounced. It has been held in the past that the transition from classificatory to comparative and quantitative concepts in science has been requisite because the objects and events around us do not exhibit the rigid boundaries necessitated by the classificatory schemata. Thus the distinctions between hard and soft, liquid and solid, etc., all seem to be of a "more-or-less" character upon closer inspection. This statement of the distinction is open to criticism. Every one of the distinctions in nature can be dealt with in classificatory terms by propounding precise boundary lines. But, on the other hand, there is no doubt that comparative and particularly quantitative procedures have advantages not possessed by the classificatory. A few of these will be outlined with examples:

(1) By using metrical concepts it is frequently possible to distinguish among instances which would be considered together *in toto* in a given classification. Quantitative terms can provide greater descriptive flexibility and subtlety. Thus the essentially classificatory scales of air pressure (e.g., 'light wind,' 'strong wind'), which used to be used in the early days of aircraft building have been generally replaced by the quantitative concept of wind speeds in miles per hour which can be exactly measured in a wind tunnel. This manifestly permits closer differentiations than were possible without the exactly regulated air pressure in a wind tunnel.

(2) Greater descriptive flexibility helps towards the elimination of rigidity in the formulation of laws. Thus by using classificatory terms, we might formulate laws such as this: "In the Summer, the leaves of deciduous trees are green; in the Autumn they turn to gold and in the Winter they become gray and die." With the help of ordering terms of the metrical type, it is possible to formulate much more precise biological laws which express the proportion of greenness in leaves in terms of the amount of nutrition which a leaf receives.

(3) A characterization of several items in terms of a quantitative concept shows their relative position much more clearly than

the corresponding classificatory concept. Thus the use of an I.Q. test may give me two I.Q.'s of 83 and 125. Qualitative characterizations, such as 'fair' or 'brilliant,' indicate no such precise relationship. (I assume that the I.Q. test is thoroughly reliable—a characteristic which is not yet universally agreed upon by educators in connection with any known test.)

(4) General laws can be expressed in terms of functional relationships between different quantities. The concepts and terms of higher mathematics and especially statistical theory can be applied to what would otherwise be quite vague laws. For example, the old fashioned economic division of society was, broadly speaking, into rich and poor with a greater and greater allowance for the place of the middle classes after the decline of the Middle Ages. Modern econometrical methods of computing the cost of living index, combined with sociological scales of authorities such as Chapin and Bogardus for assessing the standard of living by the person-to-room ratio and other procedures, have applied highly elaborate computational methods with subtle results to what used to be a very crude economic classification.

(5) Quantitative methods provide a very convenient supply of adjectives. Qualitative and quantitative distinctions exist between two forms of language, and not between two types of nature. Since so many quantitative results are given in numerical form, and numbers serve in natural languages in the capacity of adjectives, it is clear that the adjective supply is virtually infinite.

The study of concept formation is the main concern of operational analysis, a scientific procedure which has received its classical formulation in the work of Bridgman.(2) Within the school of operational analysis the term 'concept' is used in a highly specialized way, for all intents and purposes synonymously with the term 'empirical construct.' "Theoretical" entities such as atoms, electrons or the ether are not claimed as applicable to the operational analyst's premises, but all other scientific concepts are. But this does not make for an absolutely exclusive classification, since what marks the distinction in many cases is how a concept is construed. Two examples

20

are provided in the cases of gas pressure and Loschmidt number. If the latter is considered as being explicitly defined by the measured variables which serve for its actual computation, then it is as empirical as pressure, though it is a more abstract construct. On the other hand, both are defined within the kinetic theory in terms that exclude them from the hierarchy of empirical constructs.

The familiar first-approximation definition of length in terms of miles for the manipulation of yardsticks makes a convenient illustration.(3) It is often considered that rules such as these are the operational definition of the concept in question and that such a set of defining operations is the meaning of the concept. Formulations such as these seem to me to be open to criticism because they do not sufficiently distinguish between the symbols and their referents. Roughly speaking, the operational definition of 'length' stands in the same relation to length as the recipe for a pudding to the pudding itself. Definitions are simply verbal conveniences which are dispensable, but serve a useful purpose as abbreviations for what might otherwise be unwieldy and constantly recurring periphrases. Pragmatically, we could not use language effectively or elegantly without recourse to some definitions. They are neither true nor false, and cannot be criticized on any formal grounds provided that they fulfill certain logical requirements. One of the major problems of operationism is that these requirements cannot be specified in any *a priori* or prescriptive manner. The best that the operational analyst can do is to point out which requirements are fulfilled and which must be fulfilled to make specific concepts pragmatically successful.

The requirements of *operationism* may be clarified by comparing them with the opposite method of investigation, by which the scientist may determine the fundamental concepts at the basis of science by definitions which refer to properties, as, for example, time was defined by Newton. The celebrated definition of Newton made time "that which from its own nature flows equably without regard to anything external." By this method of determining concepts, the investigator is led to depend on preconceptions which may or may not correspond to anything in existence, a dependency of which Newton was perfectly aware.

The *operationist* has no recourse to such procedures. His aim is to express concepts in purely functional terms, i.e., in terms of the

21

operations by which the properties referred to by the concepts may be quantitatively determined. To define time operationally is to give an account of the operations by which simultaneity, durations and time differences are actually measured, and in this way he is guided solely by experimental facts. Einstein is possibly more responsible than any other physicist for the tendency towards the operational viewpoint, since the revision of concepts made by relativity did involve a scrutiny of the actual operations by which measurements are made, and an endeavor to bring concepts more closely into relation with those operations.

An operational definition is the verbal account not only of certain manipulations, but also of computations. It often has a rather complicated logical form. (4) Bridgman's thesis was that we know what a concept means only if we are able to identify an instance of it, and this always involves the performance of an operation of some kind or another, however small. Thus he writes:

> "We evidently know what we mean by length if we can tell what the length of any and every object is, and for the physicist nothing more is required. To find the length of an object, we have to perform certain physical operations. The concept of length is therefore fixed: that is, the concept of length involves as much as and nothing more than the set of operations by which length is determined. In general, we mean by any concept nothing more than a set of operations; *the concept is synonymous with the corresponding set of operations.*" (5)

If a concept is synonymous with a set of operations, then the fact that the scientist reaches the same "number" as a result of performing various types of operation of measurement should not justify him in using the same name to describe the different operations. And if the "number" is sufficiently important for him to use the same name in relation to his various operations whenever he reaches the same "number", does not this indicate that the concept is *not* identical with the operations by which the number is determined? An illustration of this is provided by the concept of length as extended to ultra-microscopical determinations. The basic meaning of the concept is optical, according to Bridgman. If this were all, numbers would be dependent for their correctness on the validity of optical theory. Obviously they are not, and to prove this we can apply what he calls "checks", e.g., from considerations of density. But if by the concept we mean nothing but the operations, why should there be any satisfaction in aiming at the same "number" by operations concerning density? If optical length is a different concept from density length, and if there is no such thing as length except in terms of these or those particular operations, what is the significance of checking one operation by another? These questions lead Bridgman to his celebrated conclusion that a purely operational view of the concept is impossible.

It seems to me that Bridgman's position presents a number of difficulties. In the first place, since a concept is synonymous with a set of operations, how is it ever possible to discover new operations in terms of which the concept may be defined? Let us suppose than an educator were to discover a new type of psychological test for the measurement of the I.Q. Is it logical to say that the test measures intelligence, when intelligence has already been defined as something which is measured only by previously existing tests? If the operation of testing is different, what is tested must, on Bridgman's theory, also be different. Whether the new test measures intelligence or not would be decided, supposedly, by observing how different the new operations were from the old. If the newly discovered test involved, for sake of argument, substituting the measurement of brain waves for the answering of questions, there would in all probability be a considerable reluctance to allow this as a measure of intelligence. If, on the other hand, the proposal were simply a new series of questions which the candidates were to be asked, it might receive general acceptance immediately. This appears to mean that anyone attempting to define intelligence operationally knows already what intelligence is, even though his concept be vague. The educator is then faced with two alternatives. Either he can leave the term 'intelligence' vague, making some definition such as 'that which is measured by existing tests, together with any other similar tests that may be discovered in the future', or he can frame a definition in terms of the tests actually existing, and then redefine the word every time somebody invests a new test. The former procedure is obviously open to the charge of vagueness, and the latter course means the indefinite multiplication of terms. Though the second alternative may seem the more plausible, it leads ultimately to a language containing only proper names, and it seems to me that Bridgman's type of operationism is committed to this.

But this is not the end of the problem. Bridgman nowhere indicates that the operational theory applies to all concepts, or even, indeed, to all concepts of physics. However, it is true that if all concepts are operationally definable, a distinction must be made between two aspects of the meaning of a concept—the object to which it refers and the manner in which it refers to this object. Thus if the concept of length is defined in terms of operations that are performed on objects, the concept of operation itself must surely be defined in the same way. The difficulty is that the concept 'operation' is explicitly operational since it means an operation. On the other hand the concept 'length' is only implicitly operational since it does not mean an operation, but something non-operational by means of an operation. Concepts which are explicitly operational are comparatively few in number, and to some extent confined to gerund formulations. The gerund implies an operation, whereas concepts such as 'length', 'mass', 'volume', etc., do not explicitly mean operations at all, and are only implicitly operational. I presume that when Bridgman speaks of operational definition he is referring to implicit operational definition. If this is the case, I agree with most of what he says, and particularly that all concepts are implicitly operational. The reason that his notion of operational definition is misleading is, I think, that he has omitted to consider the explicit varieties of this type of definition.

Even so, a further restriction seems apparent. If anything A is relative to something S, we can only know this fact by having some knowledge of both A and S and the relationship between them. If concepts are relative to operations, as Bridgman maintains, and if, as I believe is correct, operations are dependent on things operated on, then concepts must be relative to things. The very fact that we know this means that we know A and S independently of the operations. Hence, Bridgman's theory must be further limited. Surely, in defining a concept which is implicitly operational, there must always be something which is given in some sense on which

24

the operation is performed. The concept refers explicitly to this object and only implicitly to the operation.

However valuable the operational definition may be, it can never replace the formal definition, since these are basically different in function. The formal definition is qualitative, the operational definition is a description of the processes involved in determining the measure of the concept, i.e. the quantitative correlate of what was provided in the formal definition. The operational definition is only valuable in certain instances. For example, force, in operational terms, is a description of the technique of reading a spring balance. But force is more than merely its quantitative correlate, and the operational conception is useful only when we know exactly what constitutes a force. Until we know this, we cannot give any type of definition to the concept of force.

In a way, the qualification "operational" is merely a matter of emphasis. Linguistically considered, operational definitions are chains of definitions of a complex form, interspersed with explicit definitions and rules for computations. Since definitional chains can be provided for all empirical constructs, operational reduction amounts virtually to a process of successive elimination of all terms not belonging to that very restricted vocabulary which is a sufficient verification basis on the thing level. This is the best interpretation of the time-worn saying that science deals with common-sense objects and with these only. It is essential, of course, that the verification basis should contain relation words, since the description of manipulations is for all intents and purposes a description of relational events on the thing level. Though the agency of the experimenter is pragmatically of the greatest importance, it is systematically quite incidental. Furthermore, the definition of an empirical construct always provides the instructions, in terms of the thing level, for determining the truth or falsehood of statements in which the construct occurs. It is in this sense alone that the operational definition of a construct can be said to be its own meaning.

My difference with Bridgman's standpoint lies largely in his interpretation of concepts. There is indubitably a logical case for maintaining, as he maintains, that concepts must be kept in the closest possible connection with the operations by which the properties they refer to are to be determined. It also seems unblameworthy to propound that a concept which refers to properties which cannot be determined by any actual operations should be regarded with suspicion. But surely it is erroneous to say that concepts mean nothing more than a set of operations.

Bridgman insists on the approximate character of empirical knowledge. Any statement about numerical relations between measured quantities, he observes, must always be subject to the qualification that the relation is valid only within limits. But what does this statement mean in terms of operations? If the successive readings of a scientist on a scale give values ranging from 14.15 to 14.17, then those are the values he has obtained, and for convenience he may speak of "the value" as $14.16\pm.01$. But if the concept is synonymous with the operation, then there is no meaning whatsoever in describing the value as merely approximate. Furthermore, it is impossible to speak of the result of an operation as only approximate except in relation to some property that is being measured.

The special hypotheses of the simplicity of nature, of the finiteness of nature in the direction of the very small and of the determinateness of the future in terms of the present are admitted by Bridgman as having operational usefulness, but are simply regarded as generalizations from past experience. They are not seen as general methodological postulates. Indeed, this criticism is typical of a good many which could be made of similar parts of Bridgman's theory. L. J. Russell has, I think, justly summed up this viewpoint in the general injunction: "When new facts come along, don't try to explain them; gather them until you are familiar with them, and then add them as new to the old store."(6) Despite its informality, this genial rebuttal is very convincing.

The criticism has been made periodically, particularly by rationalists,(7) that operationism reduces physics to mere pointer readings. Admittedly, point-pointer coincidence is itself relational, and so this basis does have more to be said for it than is sometimes allowed. Nevertheless, this criticism does seem to savor of overreductionism. There is no manifest reason why the construction of the vocabulary which is necessary for a physicist's recognition of the apparatus whose pointer positions he reads and his identification of the experimental set-up could not be achieved from a basis as restricted as that of space-time axiomatics founded on coincidence. But looking at the problem from the opposite point of view, relationships different from the point-pointer coincidence would· presumably have to be shown to be reducible to this nucleus to validate its being a sufficient verificational basis. In any case, the definitions of empirical constructs do contain calculational elements, and these cannot be identified with symbolic elaboration, still less put in opposition to an operationism thus overnarrowly conceived.

Operational analysis arranges empirical constructs in a hierarchy which rests upon the verification basis, and Bergmann(8) has suggested that the direction from the verification basis might be visualized vertically and spoken of as one degree of abstractness. He holds that there is no methodological reason for making any "horizontal cut" within the empirical hierarchy, so that the terms above such an arbitrary line would be in some strange sense theoretical, whilst those below would not. If the hierarchy of the empirical constructs is the unitary structure that the operational analysis makes it, then the referents of the empirical constructs are as real as material things.

A periodical criticism of Bergmann's synthesis argues that the hierarchy is impossible to visualize, since a single concept can be given an almost infinite number of operational definitions. Who, for example, will seriously suggest that there is one operational definition of 'atomic power' or 'electric current'? Bridgman's distinction between yardstick length and surveyor's length on the one hand and the length of astronomy and that of atomic physics on the other is here most applicable. The empirical laws which hold good between the referents of the empirical constructs support Bergmann's standpoint. We may find three different constructs for electric current by way of example:

(1) 'Current as measured by the deviation of a magnetic needle.'
(2) 'Current as measured by its thermic effects.'
(3) 'Current as measured by sedimentation out of an electrolytic solution.'

These constructs are concomitant, as a matter of empirical law, and are in a perpetual, quantitative relation. It is thus perfectly possible to visualize not only the hierarchy, but different levels within it.

27

No one will deny that empirical constructs which, under specific conditions remain constant in time, can be applied to the world around us. With regard to constructs which manifest no such constancy, we have succeeded in connecting them with temporal invariants by empirical laws in which time has no place. These two types of constructs show the difference between temporal constancy (i.e., a law about constructs), and the specificity which their operational definitions should possess. Constancy is either temporal or it refers to the recurrence of situations in which constructs are applicable. Having arrived at this conclusion, one has reached a level which can be dealt with only by the techniques of the empiricist epistemology which are the present-day equivalent of the old-fashioned categorical analysis. The tendency, which is still occasionally seen, of dealing with general features of the actually obtaining lawfulness in the analysis of concept formation is surely a last remaining vestige of the transcendental deduction propounded by Kant, and which is now generally obsolete.

Since the idea of an operational definition is in some respects analogous to what other authors refer to as a semantical rule, it is suitable to compare Bridgman's position with that of more recent writers. Many authorities today would divide physical theory into three essential parts. First, there are the equations of the theory, e.g., Newton's equations of motion, Maxwell's equations of the electromagnetic field, etc. These equations contain terms like 'time,' 'force,' 'magnetic field intensity,' etc. By themselves they cannot be checked to see whether they are in agreement with the physical facts or not. Nor are we in a position to check their logical consistency. These equations are best referred to as the calculus of the field of physics. Thus we can correctly speak of Newton's equations of motion as the calculus of mechanics. These equations have as their basis a second calculus by which we can learn what transformations of our equations are to be allowed without any alteration in their meaning. Mechanics needs as a basis, the calculus of algebra and geometry. It is only by the application of this second calculus that the consistency of the first can be checked. In addition to equations and logical rules we should add thirdly statements which define the physical meaning of words like 'time,' 'force,' 'mass,' etc. It is these statements, containing words like 'warm water,' 'iron bar,' 'wooden cube,' etc., which are generally referred to as semantical rules. These rules are not unambiguously determined by the facts. Supposing that a certain word in a fictitious object-language were used in 96 per cent of cases for the sun and in 4 per cent for electriciy. It is then a matter of our own decision whether we construct the rules in such a way that both the sun and electricity are designata of the word in the object-language or only the sun. If we chose the first, the use of our object-language word was right in 4 per cent of cases, with respect to the rules. If we chose the second, it was wrong. The facts never determine whether the use of a certain expression is right or wrong, but only how it occurs and how often it leads to the effect intended. In science, as in any other inquiry, a question of right or wrong must refer to a system of rules.

Semantical rules connect our equations or our calculus with the words of the language of our daily life. But to avoid any ambiguity, the scientist should be sure never to apply these words in a wider domain than in the range of their applications in daily life. For example, it could be illegitimate to apply the expression 'wooden cube' to a body of one million cubic miles, for we do not know whether the existence of a wooden cube of these dimensions would violate the laws of physics. The same precaution has to be taken in using words such as 'time' or 'distance.' As Carnap(9) maintains, it is only by adding these semantical rules to the equations that the latter become physical laws which can be checked by experiments.

A discussion of this topic would be most incomplete without at least some reference to the school of thought known as convention-alism, of which Poincaré(10) was the leading spokesman. The con-ventionalists, for the most part, assumed that eventually scientists will find for any set of equations a set of operational definitions which could be added to these equations with a view to turning them into confirmed physical laws. If operational definitions of some of the symbols in the equations were given, the equations would become operational definitions of the rest of the symbols. Thus Newton's equations of motion would no longer be laws of motion. If we were to add to them the operational definitions of 'acceleration' and 'mass,' the equations would become operational definitions of 'force' or a convention dictating the use of the term 'force.'

Poincaré was more exact in his delineations than most of his followers. He emphasized that an experimental confirmation of equations plus operational definitions does not confirm the equations, and that, by admitting any imaginable operational definition, we can turn every equation into a confirmed one. If we consistently differentiate between what Poincaré calls "simple and practical" operational definitions and arbitrary definitions, it becomes clear that in a sense the general laws of physics may be described as purely conventional. Equations, by themselves, are only valid by experiment if, by substituting "simple and practical" operational definitions, they become confirmed physical laws. An operational definition is "simple and practical" if there are physical laws according to which the numerical result of this definition is identical with the result of other independent operations.

The advocates of conventionalism have in the principle of the conservation of energy an illustration which has received some approval. We presume in the first instance that only mechanical and heat energy play a part. In the case of an isolated system we can say that the sum of heat energy H and mechanical energy M remains constant through all interchanges, or in mathematical terms: $H+M$ = Constant. If electromagnetic phenomena come into play this is no longer true, and so we introduce a new symbol for electromagnetic energy E. The mathematical formulation will now read: $H+M+E$ = Constant. If the last equation is not confirmed by experiment, we can always add a term U for unknown energy in such a way that the equation $H+M+E+U$ = Constant is confirmed by experiment. In this instance the operational definition of the term U is contained in the equation. However, electromagnetic energy E has not been defined by the equation of conservation only, for we can also calculate E operationally from the electric and magnetic field intensity. To say that both the definitions of E which we possess render one and the same result means to assert the validity of a specific physical law. This law gives a practical value to the introduction of E, whereas the introduction of U would be practical only if we knew a second operational definition of U which is independent of the conservation equation $H+M+E+U$ = Constant. Then the principle of the conservation of energy would be a statement about facts and would no longer be purely conventional.

In their exploratory pretheoretical research, scientists will often

30

have to avail themselves of the vocabulary of conversational language with all its imperfections and drawbacks. But in its development, physics will have to modify its conceptual apparatus so as to enhance the theoretical import of the resulting system and the precision and uniformity of its interpretation, without being encumbered by the consideration of preserving the prescientific use of conventional terms taken over into its vocabulary. At the present day the connection between the technical and prescientific meaning of some theoretical terms has become quite tenuous. This has not been a loss in the long run, so much as a gain. The singular benefit of this type of linguistic alienation is manifested constantly in the increase in the scope, simplicity and experiential confirmation of scientific theories.

III

QUANTITATIVE INDUCTIVE PROCEDURES

Deductive and inductive procedures seem to me to be analogous in all vital respects. Any reasoning or inference in philosophy and science leads to a conclusion which is either necessarily true or not. The first type of conclusion is that of deductive inference and its most typical manifestations are to be found in the conclusions of pure mathematics. All nondeductive procedures I group under the general category of inductive inference.

Judgments of an inductive nature are based fundamentally on evidence leading to a hypothesis. Hypotheses are of various types, e.g.:

(1) Single events, e.g. the weather tomorrow or who will be the next President.
(2) General trends, e.g., the rise in population or how favorable or unfavorable trade balances will develop.
(3) Laws, e.g. in physics or physiology.

The philosopher takes as a basis the observational evidence at hand and from it decides whether or not to reject the hypothesis. Naturally the philosopher knows that his decision is under no circumstances infallibly true. When fresh evidence is available he may have to revise or even abandon his original hypothesis. If the evidence is favorable, his hypothesis is confirmed more strongly than before, and if the increase in the degree of confirmation is sufficiently encouraging, he may make a specific decision on future procedure.

Instead of merely examining a hypothesis, the philosopher may attempt the formulation of quantitative estimates for the unknown value of a particular magnitude. He may wish to estimate the *amount* of rain that will fall tomorrow, the *number* of eligible candidates for the presidency or the *rate* in the growth of population numbers as reflected in demographic statistics. When the philosopher is examining the evidence to discover if it is more or less favorable, I imply that he uses a *method of confirmation*, and when he applies a quantitative procedure, I imply that he uses a *method of estimation*.

Before attempting to justify any axioms in inductive logic, it is imperative to justify the existence of quantitative inductive logic, since some authors have declared it a completely invalid procedure. Kries,(1) for example, points out that there are very many different factors determining the choice of the most acceptable hypothesis, and some of them cannot be evaluated numerically. Even the logical factors such as the extension, precision and variety of the conforming material are generally inaccessible to numerical evaluation and, in any case, it is impossible to define a quantitative degree of confirmation dependent upon these factors. Nagel(2) has elaborated on the various factors which a scientist has to consider when accepting or rejecting a hypothesis based on observational evidence, and doubts whether it is possible to arrange hypotheses in a linear order of increasing confirmation on the basis of any given evidence.

In answering these objections it is essential to differentiate between inductive logic *qua se* and the methodology of induction. The latter provides no exact rules but only guidance as to how best to apply inductive procedures in any given circumstances. The conspectus of inductive logic, on the other hand, virtually covers the proofs and applications of all possible theorems on the degree of confirmation. But inductive logic alone cannot provide the best hypothesis on any given evidence. This can only be ascertained with reference to subjective factors utilized in conjunction with methodological and purely logical procedures. The task of inductive logic is not to embrace these extra-logical factors.

The critics of quantitative inductive logic have frequently urged that it is often impossible to give numerical values to the factors under discussion. The problem involves the counting of a number of confirming and of disconfirming cases for any given universal hypothesis h in a given observational report a. Let h be a simple law, where 'M' and 'M^1' are molecular predicates:

$$`(x)\,(Mx \supset M^1x)`$$

Let us suppose that h says that all men are rational animals. Let i be '$Mb \cdot M^1b$' ('b is a man who is a rational animal'). Then it seems logical to call b a confirming case for the law h. If j be '$Mc \cdot \sim M^1c$' ('c is a man who is not a rational animal'), then again it seems plausible to describe c as a disconfirming case for h. But suppose i^1 be '$\sim Md \cdot \sim M^1d$' ('d is a non-man who is not a rational animal'). Though it may seem plausible *prima facie* that d is an irrelevant case of h, it can be shown to be a confirming case for h^1 if we take h^1 to be the law

$$\text{'}(x)\,(\sim M^1x \supset \sim Mx)\text{'},$$

since i^1 has the same relation to h^1 as i to h. h and h^1 are L-equivalents, and so any observation must confirm or deny them as a couple and not singularly. But if somebody testing the efficiency of the law were to find a non-man (e.g. a piece of green cheese), and were to make the observation that it is not a rational animal, he would probably not class this as a confirming case for the law.

This curious situation is usually referred to as Hempel's paradox.(3) Hempel has shown that a specific definition for the concept of confirming case can be used to overcome this difficulty, and from Hempel's definition the concept of a disconfirming case is immediately definable. The observational report a can then be shown to have a specific number of confirming and disconfirming cases, a measure for the degree of variety in the distribution of the cases, and consequently a numerical evaluation of the extension and variety of empirical confirmation. It is thus not impossible, as Kries indicated that it was, to define a quantitative degree of confirmation dependent on logical factors such as the extension, precision and variety of the confirming material. In all the questions involved in the problem of degree of confirmation, the difficulty does not seem to be that there is no adequate function. It seems rather to lie in the making of a choice among an infinite number of functions, a procedure which cannot, of course, be entirely arbitrary.

We proceed now to the construction of an axiom scheme for quantitative inductive logic. A paradigm of fundamental axioms appears on page 35. All of the axioms will be discussed in some detail.

It will be appreciated that this is not an axiom system of the traditional kind, the signs of which are interpreted, nor is it a calculus, the signs of which are left uninterpreted and the rules of which are entirely syntactical. This is more in the nature of a semiformal semi-interpreted selection in which the customary interpretation of the logical terms is tacitly presupposed. It is not intended to be definitive and I trust that it will be regarded as of an experimental and tentative nature.

1. Range of Values	
2. L-implication	Quantitative
3. Special Addition	Axioms
4. General Multiplication	
5. L-equivalent Arguments	
6. Regularity	
7. Symmetry Respecting Individuals	
8. Symmetry Respecting Any Families	Axioms of
9. Symmetry Respecting Equi-sized Families	Invariance
10. Independence of All Individuals	
11. Independence of All Families	
12. Experiential Learning	
13. Meaning Postulates for F	Axioms of
14. Predictive Irrelevance	L_F

Scheme of Fundamental Axioms for
Quantitative Induction

The only precise formulations of inductive axiom schemata that are generally acceptable are the so-called quantitative axioms (A1—A4). Axiom systems put forward by modern logicians, notably Jeffreys,(4) Mazurkiewicz,(5) Hosiasson,(6) Von Wright,(7) Carnap, (8) Kneale, (9) and Shimony (10) differ as regards these first four axioms only in very minor particulars. These axioms apply to any sentence e and h in a given language L, which may be finite or infinite, and may then be symbolized as follows:

A1. Range of Values. $0 \leqq C(h/e) \leqq 1$.
A2. L-implication. If $\vdash e \supset h$ then $C(h/e) = 1$.
A3. Special Addition.
   If $e \& h \& h'$ is L-false, then $C(h \vee h'/e) = C(h/e) + C(h'/e)$.
A4. General Multiplication.
   $C(h \& h'/e) = C(h/e) \times C(h'/e \& h)$.

In these and subsequent axioms C symbolizes the concept of degree of confirmation, and in virtue of the meaning of C, these axioms may be claimed to be analytically and self-evidently true.

35

This claim has been challenged from time to time, usually on the ground that it is not self-evident that A1—A4 are simultaneously satisfied by an adequate confirmation function. Kemeny (11) has questioned axiom A4 in particular, maintaining that it is an immediate consequence of this axiom that $C(h/e)$ can be expressed as a ratio of *a priori* probabilities. If $C_0(h)$ denotes $C(h/t)$ where t is analytic, then

$$C(h/e) = \frac{C_0(h\&e)}{C_0(e)} .$$

The whole problem of confirmation is thus reduced to the finding of a C_0-function—a fact which is counter-intuitive. Helmer, Hempel and Oppenheim have also rejected A4, but it would seem that they did so only with reference to the degree of confirmation. Few critics have seriously questioned the validity of A4 as applied to frequency concepts. Kemeny states that this is the only axiom in which learning from experience enters, a principle affecting degree of confirmation but not frequency procedures.

With regard to learning from experience, discussion will recur in connection with the Axiom of Experiential Learning. Quite apart from this aspect of the problem, it seems to me that most, if not all, of the objections to applying A4 to degree of confirmation are eradicated if the concept C is sufficiently restricted. An example in the metalanguage will illustrate this. Let us suppose that '$C(h/e)$ $=m/n$' only when there is a set of alternatives $h_1 \ldots , h_n$ such that $e \mapsto (h_1 \text{ v} \ldots \text{ v } h_n)$, $e \mapsto \sim (h_j \& h_k)$ for $j \neq k$ and h_j and h_k are equally confirmed on e for all j and k between l and n, and h is equivalent to the disjunction $h_{l_1} \text{ v} \ldots \ldots \text{v} h_{l_m}$ of m of the alternatives $h_1, \ldots \ldots , h_n$.

This last argument will easily be recognized as of Laplacian origin. One criticism which could be leveled against it is that it utilizes the intuitive meaning of this concept in situations where h and e cannot be analyzed in the Laplacian fashion. The attempt of Jeffreys and Wrinch(12) to overcome this difficulty by proving the axioms for a class of arguments satisfying the Laplacian conditions, and then claiming that it is natural and convenient to extrapolate the domain of these axioms to arguments not satisfying the Laplacian conditions, seem to constitute an unconvincing inductive inference.

An excellent justification of A1—A4 has been given by Cox. (13) From the two original assumptions

(1) $C(h\&h'/e) = F(C(h/e), C(h'/h\&e))$
(2) $C(\sim h/e) = S(C(h/e))$

he derives the quantitative axioms for some functions possessing continuous second derivatives, the so-called moderately well-behaved functions. So far I have not seen any invalidating criticism of Cox's procedure, nor do I believe that his methods are open to more than minor objections.

A radically different, but nevertheless equally valid, justification of A1—A4 has been provided by Ramsey and DeFinetti, (14) both of whom worked out independently a subjective theory of confirmation. According to this concept, the degree of confirmation of h and e is determined with equal validity by every person according to his own habits for forming beliefs. This is in marked contradistinction to most other methods where the degree of confirmation is determined by the logical relations between the two sentences. The factor which both authors insist on is coherence, a natural extension of the requirement that the set of beliefs of a rational person should be internally consistent. A1—A4 are justified as being necessary conditions for the coherence, and hence the rationality, of all belief-formation procedures.

Developing the work of Ramsey and DeFinetti, I differentiate between two types of coherence, general and strict. Let us suppose that a man M is willing to accept any system of bets in which all the betting quotients are equal to the values of the function C. This function would obviously be unsuitable if there were a betting system such that M would suffer a loss in every logically possible case. If no such betting system exists, I call C an example of *general coherence*. If there is no betting system such that M would lose in at least one possible case and would not gain in any possible case, I call C an example of *strict coherence*. Furthermore, it can easily be proved with reference to an interpreted language L, that C is a general coherent C-function for $L = D_f$ there is no betting system in L in accordance with C for which loss is necessary. This is tantamount to saying that for every betting system there is a possible outcome without loss. Furthermore C is a strictly coherent C-function

37

for $L = D_f$ there is no betting system in L in accordance with C for which loss is possible and gain impossible. This is tantamount to saying that for every non-vacuous betting system there is a possible outcome with gain. If C is strictly coherent, it is also generally coherent.

Every generally coherent C-function satisfies A1—A4, and, incidentally, A5. If C were to violate at least one of the axioms A1—A5, there would then be a betting system in accordance with C for which loss would be necessary. If C were to violate A6 there would then be a betting system in accordance with C for which loss would be possible and gain impossible. I conclude, therefore, that every strictly C-function satisfies A1—A6. Every C-function in L which satisfies A1—A5 is generally coherent in L. Every C-function in L which satisfies A1—A6 is strictly coherent in L. Validations for these general assumptions have been provided by Ramsey, DeFinetti and Shimony and I presume that these are well known. I do not believe that an analagous validation is possible for any further axioms.

A5, L-Equivalent Arguments, may be symbolized thus:

$$\text{If } \vdash e \equiv e' \text{ and } \vdash h \equiv h' \text{ then } C(h/e) = C(h'/e').$$

This axiom is, strictly speaking, only necessary for those formulations of inductive procedure which use propositions rather than sentences as argument expressions. In every case L-equivalent sentences express the same proposition. The differences between the two procedures are based largely on the personal choice between a modal logic in an intensional object language and a theory of L-concepts within semantics. This distinction need not constitute a stumbling block on any account, since propositional procedures can quite easily be translated into sentential procedures and *vice versa*.

A6, Regularity, may be symbolized thus with reference to a finite domain of individuals:

$$C(h/e) = 1 \equiv \vdash e \supset h.$$

This axiom is virtually a convention, though it has been strangely omitted by most authors. It corresponds to C53-3 in Carnap's *Logical Foundations of Probability* with which, as he demonstrates, all adequate explicata of quantitative confirmation are in accord.

The Axioms of Invariance (A7-A11) constitute a refinement and a restatement of the classical Principle of Indifference. They may be formulated thus:

A7. Symmetry Respecting Individuals.

$C(h/e)$ is invariant respecting any permutation of the individuals.

A8. Symmetry Respecting Any Families.

$C(h/e)$ is invariant respecting any permutation of the predicates of any family.

A9. Symmetry Respecting Equi-sized Families.

$C(h/e)$ is invariant respecting any permutation of equi-sized families.

A10. Independence of All Individuals.

$C(h/e)$ is independent of the existence of all families, except those occurring in h and e.

Before discussing the Principle of Indifference, I shall outline briefly my concept of symmetry. Those C-functions which treat all individuals on a par I take to be symmetrical. All symmetrical C-functions fulfill the general requirement of invariance inasmuch as the value of the symmetrical C-function for two sentences does not change if the individual constants occurring in the sentences are replaced by others. Henceforth it is assumed that C satisfies A1-A7 and hence is regular and symmetrical.

In A7—A11 I have restored certain areas of the Principle of Indifference which were criticized and abandoned by Keynes (15). This has been possible largely as a result of a reinterpretation of the classical theory. I regard it as an uninterpreted axiom system with 'equipossible cases' as an undefined primitive term without interpretation. This change has been forced on modern logicians by the discovery that the older interpretation, based on the concept of equipossible cases, leads to a contradiction. The newer view uses an uninterpreted axiomatic definition, and with this as a foundation, the axioms A7—A11 remain consistent under any circumstances.

Even those authors who reject the classical Principle of Indifference should be able to accept A7—A11. This type of question is often asked. If there are p observed objects and amongst them p_1 have been found to have the property R and $p_2 = p - p_1$ with non-R, what is the probability that another object has the property R on the basis of the evidence? It is surely ridiculous to assume that the value of the probability on the evidence put forward also depends on the question of who did the observing and which particular p individuals were observed. Almost all authors, whatever their position on the question of the Principle of Indifference, take it for granted that in questions such as this the statement of the numbers is what matters and not who or which the particular individuals are. Almost everybody will agree, therefore, that no concept can be taken as an adequate explicatum for the degree of confirmation without the prior characteristic of symmetry.

The Principle of Experiential Learning may be formulated thus: Other things being equal, the more frequently a kind of event has been observed, the more probable is its occurrence in the future. This definition is almost, but not quite, synonymous with what Carnap has termed the Axiom of Instantial Relevance.(15) Let us suppose that e is non-L-false and non-general, and i and h are full sentences of the same factual, molecular predicate M with distinct individual constants not occurring in e. A12, Experiential Learning, may then be symbolized thus:

(1) $C(h/e\&i) \not< C(h/e)$.
(2) $C(h/e\&i) \neq C(h/e)$.

Using the so-called straight rule, I presume that i is irrelevant for h if e is a conjunction of full sentences of M. In this case both c-values are 1.

The last two axioms A13 and A14 both refer to a language L_F whose primitive predicates are the k predicates 'P_1', ... ,'P_k' of a family F, in which $k \geq 2$. A sentence in L_F may contain an infinite number of individual constants but no variables. e_F is an individual distribution for s individuals respecting F with the cardinal numbers $s_i (i = 1, \ldots\ldots, k)$. $h_1 \ldots\ldots, h_k$ are full sentences of 'P_1', $\ldots\ldots$, 'P_k', respectively, with the same individual constant which does not occur in e_F.

A13, Meaning Postulates for F, may be symbolized thus:

(1) $\vdash h_1 \text{ v } h_2 \text{ v } \ldots .\text{v } h_k$.
(2) If $i \neq j$, $h_i \& h_j$ is L-false.

For any C-function C and any k, there is a representative mathematical function C_k of k arguments such that for any e_F

$$C(h_1/e_F) = C_k(S_1; S_2, \ldots, S_k).$$

40

The same procedure holds good analogously for h_2, etc. C_k is invariant respecting any permutation of the k-1 arguments following the first. It is not difficult to prove from A13(1) that

$$\sum_{i=1}^{k} C(h_i/e_F) = 1$$

and from this that

$$\sum_{i=1}^{k} C_k(S_i; S_1, \ldots, S_{i-1}, S_{i+1}, \ldots S_k) = 1.$$

Now let e_1 be formed from e_F by replacing each predicate except P_1 with $\sim P_1$. Hence e_1 is an individual distribution for the s individuals respecting the division $P_1/\sim P_1$, with the cardinal numbers s_1 and $s-s_1$. $e_2, \ldots \ldots, e_k$ are formed analogously. For the given k, $c(h_1/e_1)$ depends only on s_1 and s, and can therefore be represented by a function $G_k(s_1; s)$. The same procedure holds analogously for $i=2, \ldots \ldots, k$, by A8. For any C-function C, and any k, then, there is a representative mathematical function G_k with that for $i=1, \ldots \ldots, k$,

$$C(h_i/e_i) = G_k(s_i; s)$$

Let us further suppose that $s_1 < s$. Let e'_1 be similar to e_1 but with the cardinal numbers s_1+1 and $s-s_1-1$. Then we conclude that

$$C(h'_1/e'_1) > C(h_1/e_1). \tag{From A12}$$

And from this it follows that

$$G_k(s_1 + 1; s) > G_k(s_1; s).$$

A14, Predictive Irrelevance, maintains that of the k cardinal numbers in s_F, all except s_1 are irrelevant for h_1. It may be symbolized thus:

$$\text{For } k > 2, C(h_1/e_F) = C(h_1/e_1).$$

This axiom is not a necessary condition for the adequacy of C, but it is usually assumed tacitly and makes for greater simplification. A14 may be fulfilled trivially if $k = 2$, for then e_1 is the same as e_F.

Though it will be obvious that my scheme owes a good deal to other logicians and to Carnap in particular, it will also be noticeable that I have differed from Carnap in one important respect, namely in making no use of the confirmation function preferred by him, c^*. The conditions that have so far been imposed in relation to c^* are too weak to exclude many totally inadequate explicata. Some questionable assumptions have also been made: the predicates of the language suffice to express all qualities of physical objects, the primitive predicates are unanalyzably simple and atomic sentences are taken as necessarily independent. The motivation of the assumption that the predicates of the language express all qualities of physical objects is that $c^*(h/e)$ can be altered by adding a predicate to the language, even though the new predicate does not occur in either h or e. Kemeny (17) has proposed, I think rightly, that this motivation be removed by imposing an additional condition on the explicatum: "for any singular sentences h, e, $c(h, e)$ do not depend on the language in which we express them." Kemeny also adds a condition of symmetry respecting primitive predicates, but this is subject to exactly the same criticism as the position which he is attempting to rectify. Kemeny's primitive predicates, like those of Carnap, only remain plausible when they are unanalyzably simple. Kemeny's additional conditions do go some way towards a solution to the criticism of c^*, particularly in the use of a constant k, which he calls the *Index of Caution*. The higher k is, the more observations of individuals having a given primitive property are needed to raise to a given level the degree of confirmation that some other individual has the property. The determination of k is still an open question. Though it is constructed differently from Carnap's λ, it has almost completely the same meaning. It also strongly resembles the construction of Johnson, (18) published in 1932. Consequently it is subject to most of the criticisms which were made of Johnson's procedure in the thirties and of Carnap's λ system at the present day. At present, then, c^* remains an enigma.

The quantitative procedure is the most efficient, and yet less has been written about it than about the others. The classificatory and comparative concepts are epistemologically prior to the quantitative, and the concept of comparative belief does not have the disadvantage of the strong idealization which is usually present in notions of quantitative partial belief on which demonstration of the original quantitative axioms used largely to depend. However, the strongest and most adequate comparative axiom system in existence, that of Koopman, (19) is perfectly capable of interpretation in quantitative terms, and is in some respects more satisfactory if regarded quantitatively. I am of the opinion that the chief reason for the present importance of comparative inductive logic is that so many of the problems of quantitative induction are controversial and unsettled. As quantitative methods become more clarified, non-quantitative procedures may lose some of the significance which is presently attached to them.

IV

CAUSALITY AND THE COUNTERFACTUAL CONDITIONAL

Two of the classical formulations of causality are provided by John Stuart Mill and Emile Bergson. Mill writes:

"The Law of Causation, the recognition of which is the main pillar of inductive science, is but the familiar truth, that invariability of succession is found by observation to obtain between every fact in nature and some other fact which has preceded it." (1)

And Bergson comments in the same vein:

"Now, it is argued, this law [i.e. of causality] means that every phenomenon is determined by its conditions, or, in other words, that the same causes produce the same effects. . . . We perceive physical phenomena, and these phenomena obey laws. This means: (1) That phenomena *a, b, c, d,* previously perceived can occur again in the same shape; (2) that a certain phenomenon *P*, which appeared after the conditions *a, b, c, d,* and after these conditions only, will not fail to recur as soon as the same conditions are again present." (2)

A considerable difficulty arising from these and similar definitions is caused by the traditional implication that the effect can be logically inferred from the cause. Schlick (3) has demonstrated reasonably convincingly that the understanding of a causal relation is not a process of logical reasoning, and that what is called causal necessity is absolutely different from logical necessity, which is virtually identity. The causal relation between two separate events is best understood by conceiving the two as being connected by a chain of intermediate events. If we look for the causal link that joins two events together, we shall be able to find only another event or a number of events. We cannot possibly find causality in this case, any more than we can find any "impression" (in Humean termi-

44

nology) for the idea of causal nexus. Kant was rightly in agreement with Hume when he spoke of causality as being a Principle of Order rather than a sort of tie connecting events. Kant further believed, I think correctly, that the human mind imposes a certain order on the events of its experience, and causality is one of the principles according to which this is done.

The principle of causality is not itself a law, as Mill and Bergson intimated, but rather a statement that all events in nature are subject to laws. The principle of causality asserts that every definite cause will have a definite effect, and a law of nature asserts which particular event will belong to a given cause as its effect. There is no exception to the laws of nature, for they hold good in all cases.

Since causality is frequently confused with determinism, it is appropriate to investigate the problem of logical determinism, as applied to the relationship between logical principles and reality. By determinism I mean ideally complete and precise predictability, given the momentary conditions, the pertinent laws, and the required mathematical techniques. The most well known formulation of this idea is contained in a celebrated passage in Laplace's *Essai philosophique sur les probabilités*. But the concept of a world-formula must not to be identified with the concept of determinism. For one reason, the application of deterministic laws to a spatially infinite universe can yield definite results only under highly artificial conditions. The case for a finite universe is more favorable, at least in principle, since it resembles that of closed systems. But even under these latter circumstances there remains a further difficulty. We do not know at present of a predicator, either human or mechanical, which can ascertain all the relevant initial difficulties. Even in classical physics there are limitations to the exactness of measurement which it is impossible to surmount. The Brownian motion of the molecules in measuring devices makes precise measurement of the values of variables constituting initial conditions either very precarious or impossible. But the assumption of the lawfulness of molecular motion was compatible with the evidence available to pre-quantum physicists. The principle of determinism may be considered, then, as a highly problematic hypothesis concerning the order of nature. As such it should be categorized as an area of inductive evidence. I take it that under these conditions the principle of induction

45

should be regarded not as an hypothesis regarding the universe, but in one of three other ways:

(1) A regulative maxim of generalizing inference.
(2) A definition of "inductive probability."
(3) A definition of "degree of confirmation."

The traditional problem of logical determinism can be answered by applying what we know today about determinism and indeterminism. It was Aristotle's contention that the principle of the excluded middle could not be applied to events in the future unless the truth of determinism is assumed. To illustrate this argument, we suppose that the universe is indeterministic, and in this case the proposition "World Government will commence in 1980" could be neither true nor false today. It would be true if and only if the occurrence of that event were determined at the present, and it would be false if and only if the non-occurrence of that event were determined at the present. Both cases contradict the presupposition of indeterminism, and therefore either determinism must be true or the principle of the excluded middle is not valid for propositions about future events.

Surely one basic fallacy in this argument is that it assumes that if we say that events are determined, the word indicates a property of events in themselves, instead of meaning merely "capable of being predicted." Indeterminism only asserts that the truth or falsity of a proposition cannot be inferred or predicted from present and past events. It does not assert that the proposition "the event E will happen in 1980" is not true or false at present. If the present is known, it does not follow that we can foretell the future, for there is no law of prophecy in the scientific sense. The future of scientific events can only be verified in the future. This does not contradict the principle of the excluded middle which states that the proposition is at present true or false. This interpretation of causal determinism manifests that logical principles tell us nothing about the truth of determinism or indeterminism in the world, since such principles are primarily rules of symbolism only.

"Determination" is surely best interpreted as "possibility of calculation," but "possibility" cannot simply apply to possibility of description by functions. After a scientist has observed the succeeding states of a physical system, he can always find functions connecting them in such a way that if one of these states is given, the rest can all be computed by means of the functions. If any sequence of events can be described by functions, then the possibility of such a description cannot be used to differentiate between causal and chaotic sequences. If it were, the principle of causality would always be true and tautologous. Causality does not mean the possibility of finding a function with particular mathematical properties, but rather the possibility of applying a function with any properties to such data as have not been utilized in its initial construction. This procedure is sometimes called *extrapolation*, and Schlick uses the phrase "possibility of extrapolation" as synonymous with causality. When the scientist says that it is possible to extrapolate from a physical formula, he simply means that the extrapolated values will correspond to the values which are really observed. The procedure of computing values which are confirmed by future experience is sometimes called *prediction*. A scientific Law is a formula enabling us to construct true predictions. The criterion of causality is successful prediction. But there is no method of establishing a scientific law as completely valid, and thereby proving causation in any specific instance. (4)

This view does not presuppose the truth of the present state of quantum physics. The opinion that I have outlined would not be affected even if physicists in the future abandon the principle of indeterminacy and return to a deterministic view of nature. At any event, this occurrence seems unlikely in the near future. Determinism can only be restored by demonstrating that the laws of nature do not impose any finite limit on the accuracy of the scientist's predictions. At present there seems to be little possibility of this type of demonstration.

The attempts of some recent philosophers to eliminate the connotation of efficacy from the concept of causality owe their historical origin to the work of Hume, who, roughly speaking, takes the position that the essence of causality is not efficacy but uniformity of sequence of phenomena. These philosophers have been attacked by Broad and others who maintain that the concept of causal sequence involves an unanalyzable concept of necessary connection and that regularity of sequence, while it may be a more or less reliable sign of causation, really forms no part of the concept of causation at all. Surely, as Pap (5) has suggested, one element of the problem which has been overlooked is the confusion of a rule of translation with a schema of translation. By following a rule of translation, it is possible to translate any instance of a given statement-form into a synonymous statement from which the term in question is eliminated. By the phrase "schema of translation," Pap means the form of a statement into which a statement of a given analyzable form is translatable, but which provides no means for carrying out the translation for specific statements of that form. "Theories" of analytic philosophy are sometimes rules and sometimes schemas of translation, and much ambiguity has resulted.

An example of a theory in the first sense is the frequency theory of probability, which is in one respect a rule for translating statements of the form "the probability that a member of class K has property P is r" in such a way that the term "probability" is excluded. (Whether the rule is adequate or not is, of course, a different problem.) In this sense also may be categorized the causal theory of meaning which claims that a statement like "'cat' means cat" is translatable into a statement about a dispositional property of the word "cat."

An example of a schema of translation is provided in the phenomenalist theory of material substance, which owes its origin to Berkeley, was enlarged by Russell in the "formal mode of speech" and described as the "bundle theory of substance" by Pap. Russell's plea was that the true meaning of subject-predicate statements would best be expressed in a language containing not proper names but quality-names, and there they would be replaced by statements asserting that a given quality is compresent with a given class of qualities. Most subject-predicate propositions such as 'Socrates is snub-nosed,' assert that a certain quality, named by the predicate, is one of a bundle of qualities named by the subject, this bundle being a unity in virtue of compresence and causal relations—or so Russell assures us.

Pap's further suggestion is that the Humean position may be acceptable even to the school of Broad if it is translated as a schema of translation of causal statements. This seems to me a definite possibility. For example, if we say: "C caused e" is equivalent to the conjunction of "C immediately preceded e" with some law of the form "every instance of C is followed by an instance of E," we have provided no machinery for carrying out a translation into a language of correlations. Two different statements may here be easily confused:

(1) A rule of translation: "It was the antecedent c which caused e" is equivalent to "There are classes C and E containing c and e respectively, such that every member of C is followed by a member of E."

(2) A schema of translation: "It was the antecedent c which caused e" is equivalent to some law of the form "every member of C (a class containing c) is followed by some member of E (a class containing e)."

The advocates of the Humean standpoint could do much to strengthen their case by admitting that Hume never meant his theory to be taken as an analysis of causation in the sense of a fixed and general rule of translation. Regarded as a schema of translation, it may stand more rigorous tests.

Even so, it is still possible to criticize Hume's position on the grounds of the subjectivism of his critical postulate, namely, that we know nothing directly except our own ideas. From this starting point, certitude about real causality can never be reached. The only causality that could ever possibly be discovered if the primary objects of our knowledge were our own ideas would be causal relations among the ideas themselves. Surely causal relations exist between objects and the mind, and between the mind and its ideas, but not between ideas and ideas. Hume virtually explains causality as a bond between ideas in the mind, when he accounts for our idea of any causality by attributing it to mental custom. Whatever his intention, he actually presents similar succession of ideas as the cause of our ideas of causality and the principle of causality. As several later commentators have remarked, such causality would not account for our belief in causality, because it would not be an idea, but merely an unknown bond connecting ideas. The only reason that Hume is able to formulate the theory that invariable succession of ideas produces mental custom, which in turn gives rise to the idea of cause, is that he is already in possession of the concept of causality gained through external experience.

The locating of causality among our ideas is at the foundation of Hume's celebrated argument against the principle of causality in Book I, Part III, Section III of the *Treatise of Human Nature*:

> "We can never demonstrate the necessity of a cause to every existence, or new modification of existence, without showing at the same time the impossibility there is, that any thing can ever begin to exist without some productive principle; and where the latter proposition cannot be prov'd, we must despair of ever being able to prove the former. Now that the latter proposition is utterly incapable of a demonstrative proof, we may satisfy ourselves by considering, that as all distinct ideas are separable from each other, and as the ideas of cause and effect are evidently distinct, 'twill be easy for us to conceive any object to be non-existent this moment, and existent the next, without conjoining to it the distinct idea of a cause or productive principle. The separation, therefore, of the idea of a cause from that of a beginning of existence, is plainly possible for the imagination; and consequently the actual separation of these objects is so far possible, that it implies no contradiction nor absurdity; and is therefore incapable of being refuted by any reasoning from mere ideas; without which 'tis impossible to demonstrate the necessity of a cause."

This argument seems faulty, however the reader interprets the notion of cause, and even if he overlooks the *petitio principii* in the statement that "all distinct ideas are separable from each other." Hume's argument amounts to this, that he can imagine a thing beginning to exist without a cause, and that consequently no argument from mere ideas can prove the necessity of a cause. While I agree that no argument from mere ideas can ever prove real causality, it seems to me that Hume's own argument against causality can be demonstrated to be no proof on the same grounds. It starts from the basis of mere ideas, or image, and the rest of it has very little to do with the subject of causality. Imagination has nothing to do with causes or with the beginnings of existence. The reference to existence lies in thought, not in imagination, for the imagination never possesses the idea of a beginning of existence. Thought judges whether a thing conceived exists or not, hence the error in the concept that the separation of the idea of a cause from that of a beginning of existence is plainly possible for the imagination. The subjectivistic postulate prejudices the whole issue as to the reality of causes before examination of the question even commences. If knowledge cannot attain to anything real and extramental, it cannot attain to real, extramental causes. The only causality it could possibly discover would be causal relation among images in the mind. For these reasons I find Hume's position less acceptable than that of Schlick and the other authorities with whom I have concurred.

The linguistic representation of causality is to a large extent bound up with the problem of counterfactual conditionals. This requires the definition of the conditions under which a counterfactual holds while the opposing conditional with the contradictory apodosis fails to hold. This criterion of truth must be established with due regard for the fact that a counterfactual, by its nature, can never be subjected to any empirical test by realizing its protasis. The truth of this kind of statement depends not upon the truth or falsity of the components but upon whether the intended connection between them holds good.

It is important in the first instance to distinguish between some different kinds of counterfactuals and semifactuals.

(a) Full counterfactuals with false protasis and apodosis, e.g.:
If Napoleon were alive today, France would rule the whole world.
Considered as truth-functional compounds, all counterfactuals are of course true, since their protases are false. Hence the following is equally true:
If Napoleon were alive today, France would not rule the whole world.

(b) Counteridenticals, e.g.:
If I were Napoleon, I would not be alive today,
and
If Napoleon were I, he would be alive today.
Although the protasis in these two cases is a statement of

the same identity, two apodoses have been attached which, on the assumption of that identity, are incompatible.

(c) Countercomparatives, e.g.:
If I had more money, I would have as much as Napoleon had.
In this case the translation of the counterfactual into a statement about a relation between two tenseless, non-modal sentences gives a protasis such as:
If "I have more money than I have" were true, . . .
even though the use of a self-contradictory protasis was not envisaged as part of the original intention.

(d) Counterlegals.
These are conditions with protases which either deny general laws, e.g.:
If circles were square, ...
or else suppose a particular fact which is not only false but impossible, e.g.:
If this circular wheel were also square, ...

(e) Semifactual Conditionals.
A semifactual conditional has the force of denying what is affirmed by the opposite, fully counterfactual conditional, e.g.:
Even if you had taken the medicine, you would not be cured
is the direct negation of
If you had taken the medicine, you would have been cured.

In short, full counterfactuals affirm, while semifactuals deny that a certain connection obtains between the protasis and the apodosis. The practical import of a semifactual is different from its literal meaning. A semifactual and the corresponding counterfactual are not contradictories but contraries, and both may be untrue. If two conditionals having the same counterfactual protasis are such that the apodosis of one is the negation of the protasis of the other, the conditionals are quite clearly contraries and both may be untrue. This statement will hold good, for example, if every otherwise suitable set of relevant conditions that in conjunction with the protasis leads by law either to a given protasis or its negation leads also to the other. The presence of the auxiliary term "even," and others like it, is possibly an idiomatic indication that a non-literal meaning is being conveyed, but spoken and written English is notoriously unreliable in this matter, and so it is only possible to posit this as a tentative suggestion.

The problem of counterfactual conditionals arises initially from the large number of cases where the apodosis does not follow from the protasis by logic alone. The assertion that a connection holds good is made on the assumption that certain conditions exist that are not explicitly propounded in the protasis. Thus in the statement:

If you had pushed the button the lamp would have been lighted,

we infer that the electricity supply was working at the correct voltage, that the connections of the switch were properly adjusted and that the button should have been pressed sufficiently hard to make the electrical connection. But we do not assert that the counterfactual is true only if the circumstances obtain. What we rather do is to take for granted the truth of the statements describing the relevant conditions, thus leaving quite vague the question of what sentences are meant to be taken in conjunction with a protasis as a basis for inferring the apodosis. Often the relevant sentences are linguistic presentations of physical laws, and the question of their correct definition is also involved.

Prima facie there would seem to be no method of distinguishing true from false conditionals. If we say that the apodosis follows by law from the protasis and *all* true statements, we encounter the difficulty that the negate of a protasis is included among true sentences, so that from the protasis and all true sentences everything follows. Various suggestions for dealing with this situation have been made:

(1) We may say that the apodosis must follow from *some* set of true statements conjoined with the protasis.

(2) We may exclude statements logically incompatible with the protasis.

(3) We may rule that counterfactuals cannot depend upon empty laws.

(4) We may include relevant conditions defined as the set of all true statements each of which is both logically and non-logically compatible with any counterfactual protasis where

non-logical incompatibility means violation of a non-logical law.

(5) We may say that a counterfactual is true if and only if there is some set S of true statements such that any counterfactual protasis P added to S in one relation $P \cdot S$ makes this relation self-compatible and leads by law to the apodosis.

None of these suggestions seems to me to be adequate and I shall answer them one by one.

(1) For any counterfactual protasis P there will always be a set S such that from $P \cdot S$ any apodosis follows.

(2) An analogous difficulty arises with respect to true statements which are not logically but are otherwise incompatible with the protasis. Thus:

If that pipe had frozen, it would have burst.

Among true sentences may be

That pipe never reached a temperature lower than 32° F.

But it is certainly true in general that

All pipes that freeze but never fall below 32° F. burst,

and also that

All pipes that freeze but never fall below 32° F. do not burst,

for there are no such pipes. Thus from the protasis of the counterfactual and the given S, any apodosis may be inferred.

(3) If empty laws are excluded, the following non-empty principles may be used in the case of the example used in (2) with the same result:

Everything that is either a pipe that freezes but does not fall below 32° F., or that is a toothbrush bursts; and

Everything that is either a pipe that freezes but does not fall below 32° F., or is a gelatine substance, does not burst.

By these principles any apodosis can be inferred from the P and S under consideration.

(4) In a counterfactual beginning

If Mr. Smith were in Ireland....

the protasis is compatible with

Mr. Smith is not in Eire

and with

Mr. Smith is not in Northern Ireland
and with
Northern Ireland plus Eire is identical with Ireland.
All these taken together with the protasis make a set that
is self-incompatible, so that any apodosis could result.

(5) Among true sentences will be the negate of the apodosis and
this may or may not be compatible with *P*. Furthermore *S*
may comprise true sentences that, although compatible with
P, are such that they would not be true if *P* were true.

These considerations lead to the conclusion that the nature of the
contenability of *S* and *P* is fundamental. But contenability is defined
in terms of counterfactuals while the meaning of counterfactuals is
defined in terms of contenability. If this is so, we can never explain
a counterfactual except in terms of others. (6) The decision as to
the contenability of two sentences must depend upon decision as to
whether or not general statements are laws. How do we distinguish
between laws and non-laws so that a law will be a principle supporting a counterfactual conditional while a non-law will not? It is
clear that the distinction cannot be drawn by reference to a notion
of causative force. Nor is a purely syntactical criterion adequate,
since even very special descriptions of particular facts can be
couched in a form having any degree whatsoever of syntactical
universality.

I have already described a law as a formula or a true sentence
used for making predictions. Rather than being a sentence used
for prediction because it is a law, it is called a law because it is
used for prediction. Furthermore, the meaning of the causal connection should be interpreted in terms of predictively used laws
rather than the law being used for prediction because it describes
a causal connection. Goodman suggests that a sentence should be
considered "lawlike" if its acceptance does not depend on the determination of any given instance. This allows us to say that the
sentence, "This book is black and apples are spherical," is not
lawlike, since its acceptance depends on the determination whether
the book is black. But Goodman has never clarified completely his
notion of "depends on." I presume that the sentence, "Either this
book is black, and apples are spherical," would be considered

55

lawlike, but this sentence raises other problems which the notion of being "lawlike" does not seem to cover.

In one of their many meanings counterfactual conditionals are not in an object language but in a metalanguage, and in this sense a counterfactual conditional is an inference statement in a given system. It says that if something is accepted in this system to be true, then something else in this system can be accepted to be true.

To discuss this, I shall suppose a system S in which there are various axioms including a statement p, which says "He has a dog." Other axioms may be categorized as $q_I, \ldots q_n$. For the system S we presume certain rules of inference, e.g., $R_I, \ldots, R_m$. Let us also take it that S is consistent. By means of the rules $R_I, \ldots, R_m$ it is possible to deduce from the axioms the statement s, which says "today is its birthday." Outside S there is a sentence r ("I do not have a dog") which is meaningful in S and such that if we add it to S and form a new system $S_I = S + r$, keeping the same rules of inference, then S_I is inconsistent. If in S we substitute r instead of p we obtain a system $S_2 = S - p + r$ which is consistent again.

Taking this interpretation, a counterfactual conditional "If p had been true then s would be true" will read:

"A system S based on p, $Q_I, \ldots, Q_n$ as axioms and $R_I, \ldots R_m$ as rules of inference is consistent and contains the statement s. There is such a statement r, which added to S gives a new system $S_I = S + r$ which is inconsistent. By removing p from S_I we obtain $S_2 = S - p + r$ which is consistent again."

Where r is known to be true we have a proper counterfactual conditional, but even if this were not the case, p and r could be two competitive hypotheses, and we should have two consistent systems S and S_2 which are inconsistent with each other. Where the additional axioms $q_I, \ldots, q_n$ and the rules of inference $R_I, \ldots, R_m$ are not specified, it may be presumed that these axioms, with the exception of r, constitute the whole of our knowledge, and that $R_I, \ldots R_m$ are the rules of first order functional calculus.

It was W. V. Quine who first stated categorically that the counterfactual is not directly identifiable with any truth-functional mode of composition but calls for a more elaborate analysis. Working from this standpoint C. L. Stevenson, in *Ethics and Language,* assumed that the force of the counterfactual conditional necessitates a definite theory of implication and that the if-then relation has a definite meaning and the compelling force of truth. It seems to me that C. I. Lewis' well-known conception of the possible as epistemologically antecedent to the real provides a basis for discussing this question. I feel dubious as to whether this type of statement can be significantly asserted:

"If *X* had taken place instead of *Y*, then *Z* would have taken place."

We cannot significantly assert an if-then statement when the if-clause is contrary to fact by entailment, material implication or formal implication, as Lewis has demonstrated in *An Analysis of Knowledge and Valuation.* Entailment eliminates both chance actions and constrained actions, while material and formal implication both lead to a complete elimination of avoidability and the working of chance. Lewis' final solution demonstrates that the if-clause and the apodosis are possible-matters-of-fact-related-by necessity, and together constitute a hypothetical statement possessing an intended should-would meaning, true independently of the truth or falsity of the hypothesis, or if-clause.

If Lewis' view is valid, it follows that contemporary theories of implication can express either the logical deductibility of an apodosis from a logical or actual protasis, or they can express a relation between an actual protasis and an actual apodosis. They cannot, however, express the possibility inherent in counterfactual conditional statements. This position is only tenable on the acceptance of Lewis' definition of a possible event, by which he means an event having empirical significance, but which is not actual in the instance under consideration though it might have been, or may be or might be actual as the instance is past, present or future. The terminating judgment "If *A* then *E*" should not be limited in meaning to an actual verification of the external world by means of the act *A* and the sequent experience *E*, for it intends the possibility of such a verification, regardless of whether it is enacted. The judgment is thus significantly asserted, for to deny the truth of it as a judgment of possibility is to do three things:

(1) to deny empirically precedent or actual instances as contained within judgments of possibility,

(2) to deny present or future confirmations, and

(3) to deny that anything meaningful can be said about the the external world.

Since, according to Lewis' principle of the epistemological antecedence of the 'possible,' the 'possible' is the *ratio cognoscendi* of the objective fact, then to deny the truth of the possible is patently to destroy the grounds of truth of all objective fact. This is virtually to say that the possible reality signified by the given is of no cognitive significance and the given alone is reality. This position is obviously solipsistic.

A further difficulty is involved when the philosopher attempts to translate any counterfactual conditional into an indicative statement meaning the same thing. A subjunctive conditional cannot be transformed into a simple alternation in the indicative. It may be false when its protasis is false and it may be false when its apodosis is true. As Lewis (7) has explained, the philosopher should be able to infer the consequent *hypothetically* from the antecedent; but, knowing merely that the antecedent of a material condition is false, or that its consequent is true, and hence that the conditional is true, he cannot say that the consequent *would* be true if the antecedent *were* true. A similar objection may be made to the simple translation of a universal subjunctive statement. Consider the statement:

"(x) if x were a glass and were dropped to the floor, x would be smashed."

If this is interpreted as an indicative universal conditional, it is true only if no glasses were ever dropped, for as an example of formal implication it means:

"(x) either x is not a glass which is dropped to the floor or x is smashed."

Such universal statements are only vacuously true, and are of little interest to the practical scientist.

A method of dealing with "disposition predicates" has been proposed by Carnap (8) which at first sight might appear to be relevant,

58

but it is strictly circumscribed and only applicable under stipulated conditions. Disposition predicates, may be regarded as abbreviations of subjunctive conditionals, but they cannot be defined by the usual techniques. Carnap does not give them a comprehensive definition, but offers a procedure of introducing them by the use of reduction sentences. His claims for this method are modest, since he admits that at best, the use of reduction sentences yields a partial determination only. A reduction sentence for any disposition term is a sentence stating a sufficient condition for the application of that term, but it provides a rule of applying the term only in those cases where the sufficient condition is realized. The philosopher may state more and more sufficient conditions, but "a region of indeterminateness" will remain in all those cases where none of the sufficient conditions obtain. Carnap admits that if a body *b* consists of such a substance that for no body of this substance has the test condition ever been fulfilled, then neither the predicate nor its negation can be attributed to *b*. Under the circumstances that neither the predicate nor its negation may be applied, the disposition term has no meaning. Chisholm (9) has interpreted this viewpoint as meaning that instead of saying that body *b* either is or is not soluble, we must say that it is meaningless to call it soluble or insoluble. Similar observations were made by Firth. (10) Though I am not fully convinced of the validity of this interpretation, it does seem to me that the statements:

"Body *b* is placed in the water at time *t*

and

"Body *b* dissolves at time *t*"

would be the components of a reduction sentence pertaining to body *b*, and are themselves perfectly meaningful.

Quine (11) has proposed that a strong relation of statements such as logical implication or entailment could be used when the philosopher wishes to formulate what is expressed in a subjunctive conditional. An entailment does not involve the paradoxes of "vacuous truth" which have been mentioned and which are applicable to material and universal conditionals and material and formal implication. The protases of the majority of counterfactual conditionals do not logically entail the apodoses, for in most cases there is no contradiction involved when denying one and confirming the other. But, as Chisholm (12) has shown, a counterfactual conditional may be reformulated as an entailment stating that the apodosis is entailed by the protasis taken in conjunction with a previous stock of knowledge. Statements which formulate natural laws are a sub-class of non-accidental universal conditions, and not merely what is expressed in a synthetic universal conditional.

Counterfactual conditionals may give further trouble if considered outside the context of their utterance. Let us suppose a conditional with a protasis of the form "if x were y." An enquirer may reasonably ask whether the supposition is that x is changed to accomodate itself to y or y is changed to accomodate itself to x. Thus, if I make the statement: "If Jove were a man he would be mortal," the reply could always be made: "No, if Jove were a man, at least one man would be immortal." I call the first of these statements a and the reply b. Since we know that Jove was considered immortal and men are considered mortal, should a or b be asserted? It was this type of problem that led Broad to question whether subjunctive conditionals about individuals are meaningful if taken literally.

The answer surely depends on whether beliefs about Jove or beliefs about men are taken as contrary-to-fact. If we suppose neither to be contrary-to-fact, the protasis would be contradictory; if we suppose both to be contrary to fact, we assert neither a nor b. Let us assume the view held by Ramsey and Wittgenstein that, "For all x, fx," is equivalent to the logical product of the values of "fx" and "There exists an x such that fx" is equivalent to their logical sum. This view clarifies the manner in which valid inferences may be made connecting particular instances with the general rules under which they fall. In the case of statement a, the statement p in the translation may be taken as "All men are mortal and there are men." If Plato and Aristotle constitute all the men in existence, p becomes "Plato and Aristotle are men and mortal." But this statement, taken in conjunction with "Jove is a man," does not entail "Jove is mortal." Hence one might conclude the use of the counterfactual conditional necessitates the preservation of an element of generality in universal statements, so that "all men" will refer to more men than those who have actually existed. But the difficulty disappears with a more careful formulation of the protasis. "If Jove were a man" should read

"If Jove were different from what we have believed him to be and had the attributes possessed by all men." The problematic inference is then perfectly valid even though statements about all men refer only to Plato and Aristotle. Most problems of this type can be solved by unambiguous, even though periphrastic formulations of the initial subjunctive statement.

One of the most influential contributions on this subject to appear in recent years was Reichenbach's *Nomological Statements and Admissible Operations* (13). Very briefly summarized, Reichenbach's position is that the phrase "if . . . then . . . ," serves in its counterfactual capacity to form a compound statement whose truth-value is not uniquely determined by the truth-values of the component statements, but depends also on general laws or nomological statements which establish a necessary connection between protasis and apodosis. Nomological statements include the truths of formal logic, forming an analytic category and certain sentences which express empirical uniformities, forming a synthetic category. Some of Reichenbach's nine requirements for an original nomological statement seem questionable and it would be appropriate to deal with a few of them in detail.

Rule 1 requires that an original nomological statement must be verifiably true, i.e. there must be a time t such that at t the statement is "verified as practically true" and at no time later than t is the statement regarded as falsified. t may occur "during the past, present, or future history of mankind." In other words, an original nomological statement must be accepted as true at some time in human history and never invalidated at any future time. It would be very difficult to demonstrate any instance of satisfaction in this case, even with a very limited inductive probability. What Reichenbach has done is to replace the customary concept of law as a true statement with an historical, pragmatic statement which is not much more reliable than the older concept. The difficulty now is that the nomological standing of a statement is made to depend upon the historical accident of discovery. The usually accepted conception of a law is that it constitutes a statement representing a universal regularity. It should therefore be true under any circumstances, regardless of pragmatic tests. But Reichenbach's analysis permits some laws of nature to be called false, even though they are "verifiably true." The funda-

61

mental flaw in this rule is that it confuses truth with acceptance on the basis of strong confirmation by available evidence.

Rule 2 requires that an original nomological statement must be "universal," i.e., it must not be equivalent to any sentence which is reduced and contains an individual-term. A sentence is "reduced" if it meets a number of syntactical requirements which are intended to ensure that it contains no superfluous occurrences of its constituent terms, and that it cannot be abbreviated by dropping some of those occurrences. An individual-term is "a term which is defined with reference to a certain space-time region, or which can be so defined without change of meaning." The most obvious criticism of this rule is that every predicate is virtually an individual-term, and hence no statement can be considered as an original nomological statement, for these now coincide with the class of logical truths. For example, the predicate 'Extended' is equivalent with 'Extended·Stratospheric v Extended·-Stratospheric'; hence it is possible to specify its meaning with reference to the space-time region indicated in the latter expression. Even if this type of specification be rejected on the grounds of its circularity, it is always possible to introduce into the language two new primitives, 'P_1' and 'P_2', which are synonymous with, but not explicitly defined by, 'Extended·Stratospheric' and 'Extended·-Stratospheric' respectively. In this case these primitives are individual terms, and 'Extended' can be defined by 'P_1 v P_2.' I conclude that no statement containing the term 'Extended,' e.g. '(x) Extended x,' or S_1, is an original nomological statement, and furthermore that there can be no such statement under Rule 2.

Rule 4 requires that an original nomological statement must be exhaustive and furthermore "unrestrictedly exhaustive in elementary terms." While Rule 2 is intended to bar laws which, by virtue of the meanings of some of their constituent predicates, are restricted to a specific spatio-temperal region, Rule 4 is to exclude generalizations some of whose constituent terms, by virtue of verifiable empirical uniformities, apply only within certain restricted spatio-temporal areas. The result is that the generalizations are likewise restricted in their application. Indeed, Rule 4 is so restrictive that any statement of the form '$(x)(Px \supset Qx)$' is disqualified if (but not only if) there exists a space-time region r such that '(x) $(Px$ v $Qx)$ $\supset$ $rx)$' is verifiably true. If, on the other hand, we follow what Reichenbach advises elsewhere and use contemporary scientific theory as a basis for judgments concerning verifiable truth, we have to infer that there is such an r for about any 'P' and 'Q.' According to evolutionary theories of the universe, to take one example of a contemporary scientific school, most characteristics are limited in their occurrence to sufficiently "late" parts of space-time.

Rules 6-9 require that an original nomological statement must be reduced and must have a form which meets a number of involved syntactical conditions. These formal impositions result in the exclusion of some sentences which are logically equivalent to original nomological statements, and seem to constitute a complex *ad hoc* device of minor importance. Surely it is in deductive consequences that the significance of nomological statements lies, rather than in their form. This fact Reichenbach is inclined to overlook.

The logical manipulation of sentences is greatly simplified if the temporal reference is made by means of a fixed co-ordinate system, rather than by the use of verb tenses. The beginnings of such a system have been provided by Burks (14) and constitute a modal method of dealing with valid argument forms. At this stage in the development of the logic of causal propositions there is no really satisfactory modal method of classifying and formulating fallacious forms of argumentation. Burks' calculus of causal propositions is obtained from a functional calculus of the first order by introducing the modal operators '$\square$' ("is logically necessary") and '$\boxplus$' ("is necessary on causal or natural grounds"), and adding the following axiom-schemata:

(1) $\square A \supset \boxplus A$
(2) $\boxplus A \supset A$
(3) $\square (A \supset B) \supset . \square A \supset \square B$
(4) $\boxplus (A \supset B) \supset . \boxplus A \supset \boxplus B$
(5) $(a) \square A \supset \square (a) A$
(6) $(a) \boxplus A \supset \boxplus (a) A$

and the rule: If A is an axiom, so is $\ulcorner \square A \urcorner$.

Though I accept Burks' standpoint in general, it is possible to make some criticism of specific areas of his synthesis. For example, the treatment of causal propositions and causal implication becomes easier and more akin to common usage if one uses the modal operator '$\boxdot$' instead of the rather unusual '$\boxplus$'. This use could be effected and introduced into Burks' system by the definition:

$$\ulcorner \boxdot A \urcorner = D_t \ulcorner \boxplus A \cdot \sim \Box A \urcorner$$

By dropping axioms (1), (2), (4) and (6) and substituting others, the system, C, for '$\boxplus$' is transformed into one, P, for '$\boxdot$'. The axioms to be substituted are these:

(i) $\Box A \supset A$
(ii) $\boxdot A \supset A$
(iii) $\boxdot A \supset \sim \Box A$
(iv) $\boxdot (A \supset B) \vee \Box (A \supset B) \supset . (\boxdot A \vee \Box A) \supset (\boxdot B \vee \Box B)$
(v) $\Diamond (\exists a) A \cdot \Diamond (\exists A) A \supset (\exists a) (\Diamond A \cdot \Diamond A)$

The systems C and P are equivalent in the sense that if the definition $\ulcorner \boxdot A \urcorner = D_t \ulcorner \boxplus A \cdot \sim \Box A \urcorner$ is introduced, the axioms of P are provable, and a comparable result holds good, *mutatis mutandis*, if the definitions $\ulcorner \boxplus A \urcorner = D_t \ulcorner \boxdot A \vee \Box A \urcorner$ is introduced into P. If these definitions are used to translate a formula from one of the systems into the other, and then into the first again, the final translation is the provable equivalent of the original formula. If Burks' outline of motivation "$\boxplus$" is replaced by '$\boxdot$', the causal principles of his argument are retained intact, but there is no necessity to maintain any of his highly complicated and rather controversial counter-intuitive principles, e.g., the so-called "paradoxes of causal implication."

Furthermore, one may disagree, I believe reasonably, with Burks' analysis of counterfactual implication. His translation of:

"If it had been the case that A, then it would have been the case that B"

is

$$\ulcorner \boxplus (A \supset B) \cdot \sim A \urcorner.$$

This translation would be perfectly acceptable in some circumstances, but overlooks uses of a fundamentally non-causal character, e.g.,

64

"If you had opened the window, you would have heard the bird singing outside,"

which is essentially descriptive, or

"If he had lost his money, he would have gone to the police,"

which is essentially expressive of intention.

It would seem that the infant procedures of modal logic have much to offer in the clarification of problems of causality for the future. Most of the work done so far in this field has been concerned with the deductive interrelations of causal and non-causal propositions. As the traditional division of logic into inductive and deductive areas manifests, there are two different kinds of relations into which causal propositions enter. To define "cause," "causality," "causal law," etc., comprehensively, the formulation of both the deductive and inductive properties of these concepts is necessary. Burks has gone some way towards the deductive formulation. The study of the inductive properties of causal propositions is a largely uncharted field, and offers high prospects for the future.

THE PROBLEM OF REAL NUMBERS

The definition of pure mathematics provided by Russell delineates precisely the area of mathematical truth with which the scientific philosopher is concerned:

"Pure Mathematics is the class of all propositions of the form 'p implies q,' where p and q are propositions containing one or more variables, the same in the two propositions, and neither p nor q contains any constants except logical constants." (1)

Pure mathematics must contain no indefinables except logical constants, and no premises except those which are concerned exclusively with logical constants and with variables. Applied mathematics, on the other hand, uses results which have been shown by the application of pure mathematics to follow from some hypothesis as to the variable and which are asserted of some constant which satisfies the hypothesis under discussion. When I say that mathematics is *a priori* I mean that all mathematical constants are logical constants and that all the premises of mathematics are concerned with these. The method of defining the logical constants themselves can only be that of enumeration, for they are so fundamental that all the properties by which the class of them might be defined presuppose some terms of the class. In practice the procedure for discovering logical constants is the analysis of symbolic logic.

The doctrine that all mathematics is deduceable from logical principles was advocated by Leibniz and developed by Frege, Whitehead and Russell. I differ with Frege in my view of the doctrine of classes, and since this concept is fundamental both to logic and mathematics, it is requisite to clarify Frege's position. His doctrine seems to me to be this. If a is a class of more than one term, and is identical with the class whose only term is a, then to be a term of a is synony- with being a term of the class whose only term is a. Hence a is the only a term of *a*. *Prima facie* this argument proves that the extensional view of classes is inadmissible. If *a* is taken as being a collection, it seems possible to make one of two conclusions:

(1) A collection of more than one term is not identical with the collection whose only term it is.

(2) In the case of a collection of many terms there is no collection as one term, but the collection is strictly many.

Conclusion (1) is that of Frege and Peano. It is an acceptable standpoint only if one accepts Frege's notion of a range as being identified with the collection as one. But, as Russell has clearly shown on several occasions, there are cases where there exists a collection as many, but no collection as one. Furthermore, the class as one does not always exist, and the class as many is of a different type from the terms of the class, even when the class has only one term. For example, there are propositional functions $\phi\ (u)$ in which u may be a class as many, which are meaningless if one of the terms of the class is substituted for u. In short, I find it difficult to see any entity such as Frege's range.

Conclusion (2) does not offer any more satisfactory a solution. We may suppose that a collection of one term is that one term, and that a collection of many terms are those many terms, so that there is no single term which is the collection of the many terms in question. But, as Russell has indicated, if *a* is a class-concept, what appears symbolically as the class whose only term is *a* will, *prima facie*, be the class concept under which falls only the concept *a*, which is usually, if not always, different from *a*. This argument can only lead to the stage where this is no one definite entity which is determined equally by any one of a set of equivalent propositional functions, i.e., there is no meaning of *class* left which is determined by the extension alone. Thus there is no way of denoting what should symbolically correspond to the class as one.

In contradistinction to Frege, Whitehead and Russell adopted attributes to the exclusion of class at the level of primitive notation, and then introduced class names and class variables by contextual definition in terms of their theory of attributes. These attributes were called *propositional functions* in *Principia Mathematica*, but the authors did not differentiate between propositional functions in this

67

sense and propositional functions in the sense of open sentences or predicates. I take it that predicates, like open sentences, are notational forms (2), and are so devised as to expedite technical discussions of substitution. At those places in *Principia Mathematica* where the ambiguously so-called *propositional functions* can be construed as notational entities, they are identifiable more properly with predicates than with open sentences. The one difference between attributes and classes, in *Principia Mathematica*, is the law of extensionality. Thus:

$$(x) \ (x\epsilon\alpha \cdot \equiv \cdot x\epsilon\beta) \supset \cdot \alpha=\beta$$

holds for classes, whereas the corresponding law:

$$(x) \ (\phi x \equiv \psi x) \supset \cdot \phi=\psi$$

is said not to hold for attributes. Whitehead and Russell's device of defining class notation contextually in terms of attribute notation is simply the procedure of making the law of extensionality demonstrable for classes without adopting it for attributes.

For Frege, attributes depended largely upon classes, and could not stand intact without the notion of classes as they can in *Principia Mathematica*. Frege spoke of attributes of classes without regarding this notion as being reducible to the more fundamental concept of attributes of attributes. When he spoke of attributes of attributes he regarded them as second-level attributes, but regarded attributes of classes as being first-level attributes.(3)

The Theory of Types is applicable both to attributes and to classes —indeed, the basic form of the theory in *Principia Mathematica* is the theory of types of attributes, or propositional functions. The type of structure is automatically inherited by classes, through the contextual definitions by which the theory of classes is derived from that of attributes. Actually, it is hardly surprising that Frege never came to adopt this course, even though it had been hinted at earlier by Schröder. (4) Frege's regular practice was to have all his classes at ground level and to avoid the use of high-level attributes. His principal method of avoiding ascent in his hierarchy of attributes was to resort periodically to classes as zero-level proxies of attributes. (5) Though he provides examples of third-level attributes, and alludes to a continuation of the hierarchy, (6) he does not in practice use any variables for attributes above the first level, nor constants for attributes above the second.

Frege's preoccupation in his later life with a generally applicable analogue of the classical extension operator as a means of solving the difficulty has been convincingly demonstrated by Quine to have been useless. (7) Neither Zermelo's set theory, nor von Neumann's, nor Quine's will accomodate the remotest analogue of an extention operator applicable to open sentences in general. Zermelo, rather than Frege, is the pioneer of set theory in its modern form, though von Neumann added an important innovation in his admission of non-elementhood. Quine's position, though resembling that of Zermelo in proceeding by selective adoption of cases of the abstraction principle, is equally indebted to Russell's theory of types. The principle, enunciated by Quine, for determining what cases of the abstraction principle are to hold good, is an adaption of a formal feature of type theory.

A class I take to be an object uniquely determined by a propositional function, and determined equally by any equivalent propositional function. Bearing this definition in mind, I presume, with Dedekind, that all the terms of a series may be divided into two classes, one of which precedes the other. (8) Real numbers, in contradistinction to ratios, are required to obtain a Dedekindian series, in order to secure limits to sets of rationals having no rational limit. Since real numbers involve classes of ratios, the ratios concerned must be of some one type, and cannot be typically indefinite. Thus several of the properties of real numbers cannot be proved without assuming the axiom of infinity, though this axiom may be circumvented by various procedures, e.g. by using the null set in ordinary set theory, by using modalities, or by using a type system with extra transfinite levels such as level ω of Zermelo.

The series of real numbers, according to strict Dedekindian theory, consists of the whole assemblage of rational and irrational numbers, the irrationals being defined as the limits of such series of rationals as have neither a rational nor an infinite limit. This outlook is the result of the extension to numbers of the axiom by which Dedekind defines the continuity of the straight line:

"If all the points of a line can be divided into two classes such that every point of one class is to the left of every point of the other class, then there exists one and only one point which brings about this division of all points into two classes, this section of the line into two parts." (9)

This definition seems deficient in two ways. First, there is a certain ambiguity surrounding the word "all." If *all* the points of a line are divided into two classes, there is no point left to represent the section. If, to eradicate this difficulty, we take *all* as meaning the exclusion of the point representing the section, the axiom no longer characterizes continuous series but applies equally to all series, amongst which is the series of integers. The axiom does seem to be more admissable if it is amended to apply, as regards the division, not to all the points of the line, but to all the points forming some compact series, and distributed throughout the line, but consisting only of a portion of the points of the line. If, from among the terms of a series, some are selected to form a compact series which is distributed throughout the previous series, and if this new series can always be divided into two portions, between which no term of the new series lies, but one term of the original series, then the original series is continuous in the Dedekindian sense. One supposed difficulty about this emendation is that it destroys the self-evidence necessary for Dedekind's proof of his axiom as applied to the straight line. I do not think this is a valid criticism, since I cannot see any vestige of self-evidence in Dedekind's axiom in the first place, either as applied to numbers or as applied to space.

Secondly, the axiom excludes two special cases. A series is continuous, in Dedekind's sense, when, and only when, if *all* the terms of the series be divided into two classes, such that the whole of the first class precedes the whole of the second, then either the first class has a last term, or the second class has a first term, but never both, however the division be effected. This term, which comes at one end of one of the two sections, may then be used to define the section in the Dedekindian manner. The first case which will not fit this arrangement is that of discrete series, such as that of finite integers, where there is both a last term of the first class and a first term of the second class. The second case is that of compact series, such as rationals, where there is not continuity, in which it sometimes happens that the first class has no last term and the last class has no first term. It should be added that neither of these cases is invariably applicable. In the first case, if the series contains a proper part which is a progression, it is only true in general, not without exception, that the first class must have a last term. The second case does not happen for every possible division. But the cases that do happen are sufficiently numerous as to invalidate the original wording of Dedekind's axiom.

Furthermore, I see no reason for accepting irrational numbers in Dedekind's sense at all. If they are irrational numbers, they cannot be greater or less than rational numbers. A real number is surely a certain class of rational numbers, and there is a real number associated with every rational number, but distinct from it. Thus the class of rationals less than $\frac{1}{4}$ is a real number, associated with the rational number $\frac{1}{4}$, but not identical with it. Indeed, such classes of rationals have all the mathematical properties that are commonly assigned to real numbers.

On these questions, my own view is much closer to that of Peano and Cantor (10) though I differ from the former in some special details. For example, Peano defines segments and says that they differ only in nomenclature from real numbers. However, he regards real numbers as the limits of classes of rationals, whereas a segment is certainly not a limit of a class of rationals. Again, Peano nowhere indicates that no real number can be a rational and no rational can be a real number. He mentions that 1 differs from the class of proper fractions, but this is not true in the case of the real number 1 when this is distinguished both from the integer 1 and from the rational number 1:1. He also mentions that the real number, although determined by, and determining a segment u, is commonly regarded as the upper limit of the segment, although in fact there is no valid reason for thinking that segments which do not have a rational limit have any limit at all. But these are comparatively minor blemishes in work which is in most essentials invaluable.

I presume that the rational numbers in order of magnitude form a series in which there is a term between any two, and I have called such a series *compact*. In compact series there is an infinite number of terms between any two, the distance between any two terms is itself a compact series, and there are no consecutive terms. Taking any one rational number r, I may define four infinite classes of rationals by relations to r:

(1) Those less than *r*.

(2) Those not greater than *r*.

(3) Those greater than *r*.

(4) Those not less than *r*.

The only difference between the group (1) and (3) and the group (2) and (4) is that the former do not contain *r* whereas the latter do. This fact, however, leads us to observe other differences of properties, e.g.: (1) has no last term, (2) has a last term; (1) is identical with the class of rational numbers less than a variable term of (1), (2) does not have this characteristic. *Mutatis mutandis* the same comments could be made of (3) and (4).

If a class of rationals has the properties of (1), is not null nor coextensive with the rationals themselves, and is identical with the class of rationals less than a variable term of itself, such a class is called a segment. Basing myself on the work of Cantor, in contradistinction to that of Kronecker, I believe that segments may be obtained from single rationals and from finite or infinite classes of rationals, with the condition, for infinite classes, that there must be a rational greater than any member of the class. This has been proved by Peano, (11) and I see no reason to reject his implication, extended by Russell, that a segment of rationals is a real number.

Not all segments possess the same properties. Some consist of the rationals less than some given rational, whilst others consist of irrationals, and so it is patently evident that segments are not capable of a 1—1 correlation with rationals. I provide two reasons for this fact, though others could be provided. First, there are more segments than rationals, and consequently the series of segments has a higher order continuity than that of the rationals. Secondly, there are classes of rationals which by definition are composed of all terms less than a *variable* term of an infinite class of rationals, but which are not definable as all the rationals less than some one particular rational. By way of illustration of this second statement, and to indicate the generality of the type of relations under discussion, I suppose that *a* and *b* be two series of real numbers, and I may then obtain in all six possible relations of *a* to *b* from various combinations on *any, a* and *some*.

(1) Any *a* is less than any *b*, or, the series *a* is contained among numbers less than every *b*.

(2) Any *a* is less than a *b*, or, whatever *a* we may take, there is a *b* which is greater, or, the series *a* is contained among numbers less than a variable term of the series *b*. It does not follow, of course, that some term of the series *b* is greater than all the *a*'s.

(3) Any *a* is less than some *b*, or, there is a term of *b* which is greater than all the *a*'s.

(4) An *a* less than any *b*.

(5) An *a* is less than a *b*.

(6) Some *a* is not less than any *b*.

In this last case, mathematics itself has compelled the distinction between the variable and the constant disjunction. Statement (6) is not implied by statement (4) since the *a* in (6) is a constant whereas in (4) it is a variable. In other cases, where the influence of actual mathematics has not been so powerful, the distinction has been neglected, and even recent advances in logical syntax have by no means settled the question.

Segments, then, form a series in virtue of the relation of whole and part, or of logical inclusion, but excluding identity. Any two segments may form a series in virtue of the fact that one of them is wholly contained in the other. In the language of Cantor, the series of segments themselves is *perfect*. Thus if we form segments of segments by reference to classes of segments, every segment of segments may be defined as all segments contained in a certain definite segment. Two properties of segments of segments may be deduced from this reasoning, and which together form the Cantorian "perfection" as applied to series of segments:

(1) The segment of segments defined by a class of segments is always identical with the segment of segments defined by some one segment.

(2) Every segment defines a segment of segments which may be defined by an infinite class of segments.

It is important at this stage to differentiate between upper and lower segments. What have been described so far are lower segments.

73

Upper segments may be defined as all rationals greater than some term of a class u of rationals, under the conditions that u should have no minimum and that there should be rationals less than every u. Corresponding to every upper segment there is a lower segment which contains all the rationals not contained in the upper segment, with the occasional exception of a single rational. When the upper segment can be defined as all rationals greater than a single rational there will be one rational not belonging to either the upper, or the lower segment. In this particular instance the corresponding lower segment will consist of all rationals less than this single rational, which itself will not belong to either segment. The class of rationals not greater than a given rational can never be identical with the class of rationals less than some other, since there is a rational between any two. Furthermore, a class of rationals having a maximum can never be a segment. In the case in question, therefore, it is impossible to find a lower segment which contains all the rationals not belonging to the given upper segment. On the other hand, it is always possible to find a lower segment containing all rationals not belonging to the upper segment in those cases when the upper segment cannot be defined by a single rational.

Any given segment may be defined by various classes of rationals. Two classes of rationals u and v may be regarded as having the segment as a common property. Two infinite classes, u and v, will define the same lower segment if, given any u, there is a v greater than it, and given any v, there is a u greater than it. If each class has no maximum, this is also a *necessary* condition. Under these circumstances the classes u and v are coherent (*Zusammengehörig*) in the terminology of Cantor. (12) Following this line of argument, Cantor further shows that the relation of being coherent is symmetrical and transitive, and that this can be done without considering segments. Hence, by the principle of abstraction, both have to some third a common relation which neither has to any other term. We may take this third term as being the segment which both define. The same basic procedure may also be used in the case of the extension of the word *coherent* to two classes u and v, one of which defines an upper segment, and the other a lower segment, which between them includes all rationals with one exception at the most. Under any of these circumstances, the usual properties of real numbers belong to segments of rationals. There is normally no mathematical reason whatsoever for distinguishing such segments from real numbers.

A possible exception to this last rule embraces the concepts of zero and infinity. I believe that these may be introduced as extreme terms among the real numbers, but neither is strictly a segment. We may construct a class of rationals such that some term of the class will be less than any given rational. In this case the class will be the null-class, since it contains no terms. This is the real number zero, but it is not a segment, in virtue of the fact that a segment is defined as a class which is not null. The real number infinity may be introduced if it is taken as being identical with the whole class of rationals. If we have any class u of rationals such that no rational is greater than all u's, then every rational is contained in the class of rationals less than some u. Again, if we presume a class of rationals of which a term is less than any assigned rational, the resulting class of terms greater than some u will contain every rational, and will be the real number infinity. The real number zero may also be introduced by an analogous procedure.

Though, following Frege and Russell, I have outlined the problem of real numbers with recourse to class expressions, I believe that it is equally possible, and perhaps even preferable, to define real numbers, and indeed the whole system of mathematics, without the use of class expressions distinct from property expressions and of class variables distinct from property variables. That it is not always necessary to have special class expressions in addition either to simple predicator signs and their combinations, or to property expressions has already been realized by many logicians. Hilbert, (13) for example, has indicated a method of representation of real numbers which is still acceptable today. If a particular, absolute real number consists of the integral part a and the real number $b(<1)$, this number can be represented by means of a functor k which is defined so that $k(o) = a$, and, for $n > 0$, $k(n) = 0$ or 1 respectively, according to whether at the nth place in the development of the dual fraction of b, '0' or '1' occurs. By excluding those dual fractions in which only '0' occurs from some point onwards, the development of the dual fraction may be univocal. It is significant also that Von Neumann and Gödel, in their later writings, do not even symbolically make any difference between predicates and the corresponding class symbols; in place of the latter they use the former.

Russell did not adopt the class symbols as individual symbols, but instead he divided them into types corresponding exactly to the types of the predicates. This formed a duplication, the necessity for which has been severely criticized. Russell himself was well aware of the fact that it does not matter for logic whether classes really exist or not, if by classes we mean anything which is designated by the class symbols. I follow Behmann in believing that the class symbolism, if it is to be used at all, should be merely an abbreviated method of writing, but that we should distinguish between extensional and intensional sentences.

The problem of the names of classes may be solved by the method of extension and intension for designators in general. The explanation for this method belongs to the field of semantics rather than to that of mathematics, but it has been outlined with clarity by Carnap, (14) and I believe that it is possible to apply a basically semantical procedure to the problem of real numbers. A name for a class, according to this procedure, should be introduced by a rule which refers to exactly one property, otherwise the meaning of the new sign and of the sentences in which it occurs is not uniquely determined. This fact indicates that a semantical rule for a sign stands primarily for its intension, and only secondarily, with the help of relevant facts, its extension. Then from a strict semantical point of view the customary use of different kinds of variables for properties and for classes is as unnecessary as that of different names. The duplication of names and variables on the first level can only lead to a much greater duplication of names and variables on higher levels. In fact, as Carnap has indicated, the duplication of variables is as unnecessary as that of closed predicators. By using semantical rules, it is possible to define all mathematical concepts in a way that is analogous to that of *Principia Mathematica*, except that no special class expressions and class variables are used.

I presume that it is possible to construct a simple coordinate language of mathematics, S_M, in which the individuals are space-time points within a coordinate system selected as a matter of convention. In such a system, it is a much more complicated procedure to choose a standard form for expression of real numbers than for expressions of natural numbers. The standard expressions must enable the user of the system to find the location of positions and the distance between any two positions with the finest degree of precision. Hence there must be an effective procedure for computing any required number of digits for the representation of real numbers as systematic fractions. For every real number there is a unique representation in the decimal system if we make the proviso of excluding decimals which contain only the figure '9' from a certain point onwards. The integral part is a natural number; the fractional part corresponds to a function $f(n)$ whose value gives the nth digit after the decimal point.

Turing (15) has defined the real numbers whose expressions as a decimal are calculable by finite means as *computable*. Though all computable numbers are real, not all real numbers are computable. Under the term *computable*, however, we may include the real parts of all algebraic numbers, the real parts of the zeros of the Bessel functions, and the number π. If, then, a real-number expression consists of an expression of its integral part, e.g., in the ordinary decimal notation, and an expression for the function f corresponding to its fractional part, then this real-number expression is computable if the expression for f is computable. Incidentally, Turing's concept of the computability of a function seems in all essential respects synonymous with Church's λ-definability, and with the concept of general recursiveness first expounded by Herbrand and Gödel.

The standard individual expressions in S_M will necessarily consist each of four standard real-number expressions, since a space-time point is determined by three space coordinates and one time coordinate. S_M cannot contain individual expressions for all space-time points, since no language with expressions of finite length can contain expressions for all real numbers. In other words, for every language S, a real number which cannot be defined in S can be given. Since terms and sentences of pure syntax are simply syntactically interpreted terms and sentences of arithmetic, every arithmetic which is to any extent formulated in any language is necessarily defective. But S_M presents a further difficulty. There is as yet no generally effective method which will enable us to decide for any two standard individual expressions whether or not their four-dimensional distance is 0. What we can do, if two standard expressions are given, is to determine their distance in the form of a computable function. Thus, for any positive rational number δ, no matter how small it is, we can establish one of two conclusions:

(1) The distance is $\leq \delta$, and hence the positions are distinct.
(2) The distance is $\leq \delta$, and hence the positions are identical, or not farther apart than δ.

It is patent that not all the individual expressions in S_M can be equivalent to standard expressions. I am uncertain as to whether or not the standard form can be chosen in such a way that at least all those individual expressions which do not contain nonlogical constants are L-equivalent to standard expressions. So far I have not discovered a convincing solution to this problem.

It should be mentioned that yet another theory of real numbers has been propounded by Fitch. (16) While allowing that non-negative real numbers may be defined in the classical way as classes of non-negative rational numbers, he postulates a second definition. This treats real numbers as exponents attaching to the relations that are the members of a class M of relations, M being restricted to relations of the following form between a and b: a is greater or less than b by an amount c, where a, b and c would be these real numbers. Thus the real number 2 would be identical with the natural number 2 for an M thus restricted. Negative real numbers would also be available, since the converses of members of M are also understood as admitted to membership in M. Fitch also claims that as a result of his theory, Cantor's Theorem, according to which every class has more subclasses than its members, is invalid.

For my own part I find certain difficulties in Fitch's theory, and am not convinced that he has provided a valid criticism of Cantor's Theorem. Fitch commences by introducing a class K' as a subclass of the class U of all U-expressions which "is very much like the calculus K" of his basic logic, so that the members of K' may sometimes be called theorems of K'. The definition of K' seems to have more the character of a truth definition than a definition of probability. Nevertheless, Fitch continues that since many classes of pairs of natural numbers, and classes of such classes, are completely represented in K', one can set up a theory of (non-negative) reals as those lower classes of rationals in Dedekindian cuts which are completely

78

represented in K′ ("U-reals"). It turns out that, for each bounded class C of U-reals completely represented in K′, the least upper bound (l.u.b. C) is a U-real. Admittedly, Fitch has made a slight improvement on Weyl's theory, but he has neglected to choose between the two cuts for a rational real. Hence his definition of equality of reals or of l.u.b. C, or of g.l.b. C, requires correction. Furthermore, despite Fitch's remarks, it seems that the non-enumerability of the U-reals should be provable, in the sense that to any enumeration of the U-reals completely represented in K′, there is another U-real not in the enumeration. However, the axiom of choice will in all probability fail to hold, and when it does not, one will not be able to pick up a sequence of U-reals from C converging to l.u.b. C. But there is yet another reason why the proposed theory of reals falls short of being a practical foundation for analysis. The consistency of Fitch's theory is not evident from the fact that K′ itself is consistent, as Fitch maintains it is. For the theorems about reals are only expressible in another class K″, and since K′ and K″ are not recursively enumerable, a consistency proof would have to apply to a suitable formalism for studying K′ or K″. There then remains the matter of appraising the safeness of the methods employed. Fitch claims that every recursively enumerable class of propositions is definable in K. But it is well known that there are often different possibilities for the interpretation of a given formalism. It is surely impossible to assign interpretations to the symbols of K, and be able to anticipate all the possible interpretations of all the formalisms involved.

A more convincing discussion of Cantor's theorem has been provided by Quine. (17) As Quine's system treats relations as classes of ordered pairs, the usual form of Cantor's Theorem violates the theory of types when expressed in the notation of the system, and cannot be proved under these conditions. But Quine directs attention to another form of Cantor's Theorem, namely that the subclasses of a class outnumber the unit subclasses. Quine indicates that this form does not lead to the Cantor paradox. True, Quine's conclusions conflict with those of *Principia Mathematica*, in which both heterogeneous and homogeneous relations are directly accomodated through the increase of primitives and the multiplication of type hierarchies, but on the other hand they do not conflict with the simplificaton of *Principia Mathematica* embodied in the systems of Tarski and Gödel.

79

Since Quine's criticism is couched entirely in terms of his own system, one will accept it or reject it as one accepts or rejects the premises of Quine's own logic.

In defining my own position on the real number system, I suppose that R is a collection of numbers, each of which can be represented by an unending decimal, in the ordinary decimal system, of the form

(1) $\pm k_1 \ k_2 \ldots k_m.a_1 \ a_2 \ldots a_n \ldots$ where each k and each a are one of the digits 0, 1, . . . , 9; $k_1 \ k_2 \ldots \ldots k_m$ is the "integral part" of the number; $a_1 \ a_2 \ldots a_n \ldots$ is the "decimal part"; and no n exists such that all digits a_n, a_{n+1}, . . . are all zero. Given two positive real numbers r and r', I define the relation $r > r'$ by using form (1) with a $+$ sign to represent r, with a similar form to represent r', but with primes on the k's, a's and m in the latter case. Bearing in mind the fact that the integral parts of these numbers are natural numbers we may specify that, if

(2) $k_1 k_2 \ldots k_m < k'_1 k'_2 \ldots k_{m'}'$ where the $<$ in (2) is that of the natural order in N, then $r < r'$. If the converse of (2) holds good —$k'_1 \ k'_2 \ldots k_{m'}' > k_1 \ k_2 \ldots k_m$—we define $r' < r$. In case these numbers are equal, we also consider the decimal parts of r. The first inequality (in the order of the subscripts), $a_n < a_n'$ (or $a_n' < a_n$), will determine the order. Thus, if $a_1 < a_1'$, then $r < r'$. If $a_1 = a_1'$, $a_2 = a_2'$, and $a_3 = a_3'$, then $r < r'$. If, however, $a_n = a_n'$ for every n, then the relation $r = r'$ holds. For the case where r and r' are not both positive, we employ the same criterion when both r and r' are negative, but reverse the order, e.g.: $-22.6 \ldots < -3.14 \ldots$, $-5.238 \ldots$ $< -5.237 \ldots$ If r is negative and r' is not negative, $r < r'$.

On the basis of this order relation, it is not difficult to prove the following well-known theorems (18):

Theorem 1: *If r and r' are real numbers, and $r < r'$, then there exists $f \epsilon F$ such that $r < f < r'$.*

Theorem 2: *If r and r' are real numbers, and $r < r'$, then there exists a finite decimal d such that $r < d < r'$.*

Theorem 3: *If $[A,B]$ is a cut of the collection R, ordered as in (2), then either A has a last element or B has a first element.*

We now consider some problems relating to real fractions. The set F of all real fractions has the cardinal number $\aleph_0$, and the collection R has a cardinal number different from $\aleph_0$ which we shall call c. It is a frequently proved proposition that $\aleph_0 < c$. Thus, although the number of elements in R is greater than the number of elements in F, there is an element of F between every two elements of R. Set theory explains an apparent difficulty. Though there is nothing surprising about such a property for finite sets, in the present case we might presume that, since each *two* elements of R are separated by one element of F, the number of elements of R is at most twice as great as that in F, i.e, $\aleph_0 + \aleph_0$ which is $\aleph_0$. The superficial difficulty is overcome by noticing that many different pairs of elements of R are separated by the same element of F.

Of much greater difficulty is the problem of weakly denumerable sets. By a D_1-set I mean one which is a denumerable union of denumerable sets, and by a D_2-set a denumerable union of D_1-sets. I see no immediate way of proving, without recourse to the axiom of choice, that a set of power $2^{\aleph_0}$ is not a D-set. (19) It is possible without the axiom of choice to show, by means of a diagonal procedure, that a set of power $\aleph_1 \aleph_0$ is not a D_1-set, and it can also be shown, by applying Lebesgue's construction of $\aleph_1$ sets of real numbers, that

$$2^{2\aleph_0} \geqq \aleph_1 \aleph_0.$$

Hence, it may be concluded, the family of all sets of real numbers is not a D_1 set. But without the axiom of choice it seems impossible to prove that there is at least one infinite set which is not a D_2-set.

A further problem follows from this assumption. Let us consider an axiom system of set theory, e.g. the system of Zermelo with Skolem's interpretation of the "*Aussonderungs*-axiom," or that of Bernays. We replace the axiom of choice in this system by one of the following two axioms:

(A1) The set of all real numbers is a D_1-set.

(A2) Every infinite set is a D_2-set.

Are the axiom systems thus obtained consistent? At present the problem appears unsolved, but it is surely important since the inclusion of (A1) or (A2) into the axiom system of set theory, in contradistinction to the inclusion of the negation of the axiom of choice, would almost certainly produce radical changes in the development of analysis, particularly as applied to the theory of measure and integration.

Perhaps more progress has been made recently in the problems of real sequences than in any other related field. For example, a number of theorems with proofs, which appear to me to be conclusive, has been offered by Henstock (20) in connection with real linear functions, and these seem to be the most significant for the theory of real sequences:

Theorem 4: *The necessary and sufficient condition on a real sequence $\{a_n\}$, in order that $\sum\limits_{n=1}^{\infty} a_n x_n$ should be convergent almost everywhere in the space Q_ω of all real sequences $\{x_n\}$ satisfying $|x_n| \leqq \frac{1}{2}$ for all n, is that*

$$\sum_{n=1}^{\infty} a^2_n < \infty .$$

Theorem 5: *A linear function $J(\xi)^{n=1}$ is bounded in the Hilbertian space σ_2 of sequences with real x_n and convergent $\sum\limits_{n=1}^{\infty} x^2_n$ if and only if it can be extended to a set of positive measures in Q_ω.*

In conclusion, it is appropriate to comment on some operations that may be performed in the real number system R. First of all, the axiom system of R may be briefly designated, with C being a set of undefined elements and $<$ an undefined binary relation between elements of C.

(A.R.1) Simple Order Axiom:
   C is simply ordered with respect to $<$.

(A.R.2) Dedekind Cut Axiom:
   If $[A,B]$ is a cut of C, then either A has a last element or B has a first element.

(A.R.3) Separability Axiom:
There exists a non-empty, countable subset S of C such that, if x yϵC such that $x<y$, then there exists zϵS such that $x<z<y$.

(A.R.4) Unboundedness Axiom:
C has no first element and no last element.

This axiom system we call $\bigwedge$. It is not difficult to show that $\bigwedge$ is categorical. If M is any model of $\bigwedge$, then M and R are isomorphic with respect to $\bigwedge$. Then, if M_1 and M_2 are any two models of $\bigwedge$, the transitivity of isomorphism renders M_1 and M_2 isomorphic with respect to $\bigwedge$, and consequently $\bigwedge$ is a categorical system.

To perform the addition of two positive real numbers $r_1=k_1k_2 \ldots k_m.a_1a_2 \ldots a_n \ldots$ and $r_2=t_1t_2 \ldots t_s.b_1b_2 \ldots b_n \ldots$, we let $r_1{}^0=k_1k_2 \ldots k_m$, and for every $nϵN$, $r_1{}^n=k_1k_2 \ldots k_m.a_1a_2 \ldots a_n$; and $r_2{}^0=t_1t_2 \ldots t_s$ and $r_2{}^n=t_1t_2 \ldots t_s.b_1b_2 \ldots b_n$; and let $r_1{}^n+r_2{}^n=s_n$. Then, since $r_1{}^n \leqq r_1{}^{n+1}, r_2{}^s \leqq r_2{}^{n+1}$, we conclude that $s_n \leqq s_{n+1}$. Since $r_1{}^n$ never exceeds $r_1{}^0+1$ and $r_2{}^n$ never exceeds $r_2{}^0+1$, we conclude that s_n never exceeds $r_1{}^0+r_2{}^0+2$. Ultimately there exists an integer N such that, for $n>N$, $n'>N$, s_n and $s_{n'}$ have the same integral parts. There will also be an integer $i_1>N$ such that, for $n>i_1$, $n'>i_1$, s_n and $s_{n'}$ have the same digit in the first place after the decimal point. It is now not difficult to prove the existence of an $sϵR$ such that for any $kϵN$ there exists an i_k such that, for $n>i_k$, s_n and s have the same integral parts and the same digits in their first k decimal places. r_1+r_2 is therefore defined as s and we may conclude that $r_1+r_2=s=r_2+r_1$.

When r_1 and r_2 are both negative, then r_1+r_2 *is* —s. If one is negative and the other positive, we find the difference d of their numerical values and attach the sign of the number which is numerically greater of r_1, r_2, to d. To do this we must define r_1—r_2 for positive r_1, r_2 and $r_1>r_2$. For each $nϵN$ let $d_n=r_1{}^n$—$r_2{}^n$ where $r_1{}^n$ and $r_2{}^n$ are defined as before. It is then easy to prove that there exists a $dϵR$ such that for any $kϵN$ there exists an integer i_k such that, for $n>i_k$, d_n and d have the same integral parts and the same digits in their first k decimal places. r_1—r_2 may then be defined as d. If $r_1<r_2$, and r_1 and r_2 are both positive, then r_1—r_2 is —$(r_2$—$r_1)$. By performing the operations with the "approximations" $r_1{}^n$, $r_2{}^n$,

83

multiplication and division may be treated in a similar fashion.

Addition and multiplication may conveniently be based on the Peano axioms, which deal with a set N of undefined elements called numbers, and an undefined binary relation, s, between numbers. (21) It can be proved from these axioms that the successor of a given number is unique: if ysx and $y'sx'$ and $x=x'$, then $y=y'$. Hence, we may use a symbol $S(x)$ to denote the successor of x. $S(x)$ is a single-valued function over N with values in N. To define addition, we define first, for all x, $x+1$ to be $S(x)$:

Def. 1. $x+1=S(x)$, $x\epsilon N$.

Then for all y we define:

Def. 2. $x+S(y)=S(x+y)$.

This defines $x+y$ for all x, $y\epsilon N$ by the mathematical induction principle. To define multiplaction, we define $1\times y=y$ for all $y\epsilon N$, and for all $x\epsilon N$ we define $S(x)\times y$ to be $(x\times y)+y$. This defines $x\times y$ for all x, $y\epsilon N$ by the mathematical induction principle.

The definition of real numbers and operations involving real numbers may also be treated in terms of cuts of ϕ and an equivalence relation. Let Γ be the class of all cuts $[\phi_1, \phi_2]$ of ϕ. If $[\phi_1, \phi_2]$, $[\phi_1', \phi_2']\epsilon\Gamma$ such that some fixed rational number α is the last element in ϕ_2', then we define $[\phi_1, \phi_2]\approx[\phi_1', \phi_2']$; and, $[\phi_1, \phi_2]$, $\approx[\phi_1, \phi_2]$ in all cases. The elements of the class decomposition of Γ corresponding to $\approx$ are *real numbers*. If R is the collection of all real numbers defined in this way, we suppose that $r_1<r_2$ for r_1, $r_2\epsilon R$ provided that, if $[\phi_1, \phi_2]\epsilon r_1$, $[\phi_1', \phi_2']\epsilon r_2$, there is a rational number α such that $\alpha\epsilon\phi_2\cap\phi_1'$. r_1+r_2 is the element of R determined by the cut $[\phi_1'', \phi_2'']$ in which $\phi_1''=\{\alpha_1+\alpha_1' \mid (\alpha, \epsilon \phi_1)$ and $\alpha_1'\epsilon\phi_1')\}$; and $r_1\times r_2$ is the element of R determined by the cut $[\phi_1^*, \phi_2^*]$ in which $\phi_1^*=\{\alpha_1\times\alpha_1' \mid (\alpha_1\epsilon\phi_1)$ and $(\alpha_1'\epsilon\phi_1')\}$. Subtraction and division may be analogously defined.

The alternative method of Cauchy sequences is also useful. Two Cauchy sequences $\{\alpha_n\}$, $\{\alpha_n'\}$ are *equivalent* provided that, if ϵ is any fixed positive element of ϕ, there is an n such that, for all $k>n$ $\mid \alpha_k-\alpha_k' \mid <\epsilon$. Let Γ be the collection of all Cauchy sequences of rational numbers. The elements of the class decomposition of Γ corresponding to this equivalence relation are real numbers.

The usual operations may be defined on the basis of the Cauchy sequences, for example, if $r_1 + r_2$ are real numbers, and $\{\alpha_n\}$ ϵr_1, $\{\beta_n\}$ ϵr_2 then $r_1 + r_2$ is the real number determined by the sequence $\{\alpha_n + \beta_n\}$.

By way of making connection with algebraic ideas, it should be remarked that the real number system is an *ordered field*, in that its structure is that of a linear continuum. A real number system may be defined as field R in which there is a binary order relation $<$ with respect to which R forms a linear continuum, satisfying the monotonic law

$$(x < y) \implies [(x + a) < (y + a)]$$

and the requirement that $0 < x, 0 < y$ imply $0 < x \times y$. From this definition all the properties of the real number system are ultimately derivable.

NOTES

I

1. Carnap, R.: "Der logische Aufbau der Welt," Berlin, 1928, p. 65.

2. *Op. cit.*, p. 139.

3. Bridgman, P. W.: "Operational Analysis", in *Philosophy of Science*, Vol. V, 1938, p. 119.

4. Burks, A. W.: "The Presupposition Theory of Induction," in *Philosophy of Science*, Vol. XX, 1953.

5. Kneale, W. C.: "Probability and Induction," Oxford, 1949.

6. *Vide*: Wald, A.: 'On the Principles of Statistical Inference," Notre Dame, 1942. "Statistical Decision Functions," Wiley, 1950.

II

1. A precise definition of quasi-serial order in the form of nine requirements has been laid down by Carl G. Hempel in "Fundamentals of Concept Formation in Empirical Science", International Encyclopedia of Unified Science, Vol. II, No. 7, University of Chicago Press, 1952.

2. Bridgman, P. W.: "The Logic of Modern Physics," New York, 1927.

3. A development of this illustration with particular reference to the behavior sciences is provided in: Bergmann, G. and K. W. Spence: "The Logic of Psychophysical Measurement" in *Psychological Review*, Vol. 51, No. 1, 1944.

4. An elaborate discussion of the linguistic structure of operational definitions has been provided in: Carnap, R.: "Testability and Meaning" in *Philosophy of Science*, Vol. 3, No. 4, 1936 and Vol. 4, No. 1, 1937.

5. Bridgman, P. W.: *Op. cit.*, p. 5. Any attempt to enumerate the many other authors who have discussed this celebrated doctrine would be too lengthy to be practical here, but I should mention my indebtedness to these publications in particular: A symposium

on Operationism in *Psychological Review*, Vol. 52, No. 5, 1945. Werkmeister, W. H.: "Basis and Structure of Knowledge", Harper, 1945. Pratt, C. C.: "The Logic of Modern Psychology", Macmillan, 1939. Benjamin, A. C.: Review of Bridgman's "The Logic of Modern Physics" in the *Journal of Philosophy*, Vol. XXIV, No. 24, 1927. See also: "Operationism—A Critical Evaluation" in *The Journal of Philosophy*, Vol. XLVII, No. 15, 1950.

6. Russell, L. J.: Review of Bridgman's "The Logic of Modern Physics" in *Mind*, Vol. 37, No. 147, 1928.

7. Note, for example: Eddington, Sir Arthur: "Philosophy of Physical Science", New York, 1935.

8. Bergmann, G.: "Outline of an Empiricist Philosophy of Physics", in *American Journal of Physics*, Vol. II, Nos. 5 and 6, 1943. Reprinted in: "Readings in the Philosophy of Science", edited by H. Feigl and M. Brodbeck, New York, 1953.

9. Carnap, R.: "Foundations of Logic and Mathematics," in the International Encyclopedia of Unified Science, Vol. I, No. 3.

10. His standpoint is expounded most comprehensively in: Poincaré, H.: "Science et hypothèse", Paris, 1903.

III

1. Kries, J. Von: "Die Prinzipien der Wahrscheinlichkeitsrechnung". Freiburg, 1886. 2nd Edition, Tubingen, 1927.

2. Nagel, E.: "Principles of the Theory of Probability" in International Encyclopaedia of Unified Science, Vol. I, No.6 .

3. Treated principally in: Hempel, C: "Studies in the Logic of Confirmation," in *Mind*, Vol. 54, 1954, pp. 1-26 and 97-121. See also *ibid*, Vol. 55, 1946, pp. 79-82. Some of Hempel's technical results were also published in: "A Purely Syntactical Definition of Confirmation," in *Journal of Symbolic Logic*, Vol. VIII, 1943, pp. 122-143.

4. Jeffreys, H.: "Theory of Probability," Oxford, 1939.

5. Mazurkiewicz, S.: "Zur Axiomatik der Wahrscheinlichkeitsrechnung" in *Comptes rendus de la Société des Sciences de Varsovie*, CI. III, XXV (1932), pp. 1-4.

6. Hosiasson, J.: "On Confirmation" in *Journal of Symbolic Logic*, Vol. V, 1940, pp. 133-148. "Induction et analogie", in *Mind*, Vol. 50, 1941, pp. 351-365.

7. Von Wright, G. H.: "The Logical Problem of Induction", Helsingfors, 1941, pp. 106-107.

8. Carnap, R.: "Logical Foundations of Probability," Chicago, 1950.

9. Kneale, W.: "Probability and Induction", Oxford, 1949, pp. 125-127.

10. Shimony, A.: "Coherence and the Axioms of Confirmation," in *Journal of Symbolic Logic*, Vol. XX, 1955, pp. 1-28.

11. Kemeny, J.: "Carnap on Confirmation" in *The Review of Metaphysics*, Vol. V, 1941, pp. 152-153.

12. See especially the article of these authors entitled "On Some Aspects of the Theory of Probability" in *Philosophical Magazine*, Vol. 38, 1919, pp. 715-731.

13. Cox, R. T.: "Probability, Frequency and Reasonable Expectation", in *American Journal of Physics*, Vol. XIV, 1946, pp. 1-13.

14. Ramsey, F. P.: "Truth and Probability" in "The Foundations of Mathematics and Other Logical Essays," London, 1931. DeFinetti, B.: "Sul Significato Soggetivo della Probabilita" in *Fundamenta Mathematicae*, Vol. XVII, 1931, pp. 298-329. See also: "La Prévision: Ses Logiques, Ses Sources Subjectives" in *Annales de l'Institut Henri Poincaré*, Vol. VII, 1937, pp. 1-68.

15. Keynes, J. M.: "A Treatise on Probability", London, 1921.

16. Carnap, R.: "On the Comparative Concept of Confirmation," in *British Journal for the Philosophy of Science*, Vol. III, 1953, pp. 311-317.

17. Kemeny, J.: "A Contribution to Inductive Logic," in *Philosophy and Phenomenological Research*, Vol. XIII, 1953, pp. 371-374.

18. Johnson, W.: "Probability: The Deductive and Inductive Problems," in *Mind*, Vol. 41, 1932, pp. 409-423.

19. Koopman, B.: "The Axioms and Algebra of Intuitive Probability," in *Annals of Mathematics*, Series 2, Vol. 41, 1940, pp. 269-293.

IV

1. Mill, J. S.: "Logic", Book III, Chap. V, 2.

2. Bergson, E.: "Time and Free Will", pp. 199, 202.

3. Schlick, M.: "Causality in Everyday Life and in Recent Science" in *University of California Publications in Philosophy*, No. 15, University of California Press, 1932.

4. This entire problem is further elaborated in: Schlick, M.: "Die Kausalität in der gegenwärtigen Physik" in *Die Naturwissenschaften*, 1931, Heft 7.

5. Pap, A.: "Philosophical Analysis, Translation Schemas and the Regularity Theory of Causation" in *The Journal of Philosophy*, Vol. 49, 1952. Some interesting sidelights on the historical development of the theory of causality, alluded to earlier in this paragraph, are proved in: Lenzen, V. F.: "Causality in Natural Science", Charles C. Thomas, Springfield, Illinois, 1954.

6. A conclusion similarly reached by: Goodman, N.: "The Problem of Counterfactual Conditionals" in *The Journal of Philosophy*, Vol. 44, No. 5, February 27, 1947. Reprinted in: Linsky, L.: "Semantics and the Philosophy of Language", University of Illinois Press, Urbana, 1952.

7. Lewis, C. I. & C. H. Langford: "Symbolic Logic", New York, 1932, p. 261.

8. Carnap, R.: "Testability and Meaning" in *Philosophy of Science*, Vols. 3-4, 1936-37.

9. Chisholm, R. M.: "The Contrary-to-Fact Conditional," in *Mind*, Vol. 55, 1946.

10. Firth, R.: "Sense-Data and the Principle of Reduction", unpublished Ph.D. thesis, Harvard University Library, 1943. Chapter VII is especially relevant.

11. Quine, W. V.: "Mathematical Logic", Harvard University Press, 1947, p. 29.

12. Chisholm, R. M.: *Op. cit.*, p. 298.

13. Reichenbach, H: "Nomological Statements and Admissible Operations", North-Holland Publishing Co., Amsterdam, 1954.

14. Burks, A. W.: "The Logic of Causal Propositions", in *Mind*, Vol. 60, 1951. A definition of causal relation based on Burks' article but differing in conclusions is provided in: Simon, H. A.: "On the Definition of Causal Relation", in *The Journal of Philosophy*, Vol. 49, 1952.

V

1. Russell, B.: "The Principles of Mathematics," New York: W. W. Norton, 1903, p. 3.

2. A view which is argued at some length in: Quine, W. V.: "Methods of Logic", Kegan Paul, 1950, pp. 131 ff.

3. Frege, G.: "Grundgesetze der Arithmetik", Vol. I, Jena, 1893. See especially §§ 23, 24, 25.

4. Schröder, E.: "Vorlesungen über die Algebra der Logik", Vol. I, Leipzig, 1890, pp. 245-249.

5. Frege, G.: *Op. cit.*, 35.

6. Frege, G.: *Op. cit.*, 24.

7. Quine, W. V.: "Mathematical Logic", Revised Edition, Harvard University Press, 1951 (This Revised Edition cleared up some of the inconsistencies of the First Edition.).

8. This procedure is sometimes referred to as the "Dedekind cut", and is described at length in: Dedekind, R.: "Stetigkeit und irrationale Zahlen", Second Edition, Brunswick, 1892.

9. Dedekin, R.: *Op. cit.*, p. 11.

10. Peano, G. "Sui Numeri Irrazionali", in *Rivista di Matematica*, Vol. VI, 1896, pp. 126-140. "Formulaire de Mathématiques", Vol. II, Part III, Turin, 1899. Cantor, G.: "Gesammelte Abhandlungen", herausg. von Ernst Zermelo, Berlin, Springer, 1932.

11. Peano, G.: *Op. cit. ult.*, 61.

12. See Cantor's articles in *Mathematische Annalen*, Vol. XLVI, 1895, and *Rivista di Matematica*, Vol. V, 1895.

13. Hilbert, D.: "Die Logischen Grundlagen der Mathematik", in *Mathematische Annalen*, Vol. 88, 1923.

14. Carnap, R.: "Meaning and Necessity," University of Chicago Press, 1947.

15. Turing, A. M.: "On Computable Numbers" in *Proceedings of the London Mathematical Society*, Vol. XLII, 1937. "Compatibility and λ—Definability," in *Journal of Symbolic Logic*, Vol. II, 1937.

16. Fitch, F. B.: (1) "An Extension of Basic Logic", in *Journal of Symbolic Logic*, Vol. 13, 1948, pp. 95-106. (2) "The Heine-Borel Theorem in Extended Basic Logic", *ibid*, Vol. 14, 1949, pp. 9-15. (3) "A Further Consistent Extension of Basic Logic", *ibid.*, Vol. 14, 1950, pp. 209-218.

17. Quine, W. V.: "On Cantor's Theorem", in *Journal of Symbolic Logic*, Vol. II, 1937.

18. Proofs of these theorems are available in this source, *inter alia*: Wilder, R. L.: "Introduction to the Foundations of Mathematics," John Wiley, 1952.

19. This problem is not entirely original for it has been touched on by: Sierpinski, W.: "L'axiome de M. Zermelo et son rôle dans la Théorie des Ensembles et l'Analyse," in *Bulletin de l'Académie des Sciences de Cracovie*, 1919.

20. Henstock, R.: "Linear Functions with Domain a Real Countably Infinite Dimensional Space" in *Proceedings of the London Mathematical Society*, Vol. V, 1955, pp. 238-256.

21. My remarks on the arithmetic of the real number system from the Peano axiom system are derived in part from: Landau, E. G. H.: "Grundlagen der Analysis," Leipzig, Akad. Verlagsges. M. B. H., 1930.

INDEX

94